Finally! This is the *most comprehensive and immediately usable* book on parenting the ADHD child yet. Dr. Monastra is a rare combination of talented clinician and master teacher who has compiled the most up-to-date and practical information to help families with ADHD survive and thrive. This is a *must-have* book for everyone who lives with or works with ADHD children.

—*Lynda Kirk, MA, LPC, BCIA-C, QEEG-D, Clinical Director, Austin Biofeedback Center, Austin, TX*

Dr. Monastra is a leading clinician–researcher in the area of ADHD. His book will be of great value to parents, teachers, and professionals who have struggled with the diagnosis and treatment of ADHD and its associated comorbidities. His book is engrossing, very warm in its concern for children, and full of insights.

—*Joel F. Lubar, PhD, Department of Psychology, University of Tennessee, Knoxville*

Parenting
Children
With
ADHD

Parenting Children With ADHD

10 LESSONS THAT MEDICINE CANNOT TEACH

VINCENT J. MONASTRA, PhD

American Psychological Association
Washington, DC

Second Printing, September 2004
Third Printing, December 2005
Fourth Printing, May 2006
Fifth Printing, May 2007
Sixth Printing, March 2008
Seventh Printing, February 2009
Eighth Printing, December 2009
Ninth Printing, December 2010
Tenth Printing, August 2012

Published by
APA LifeTools
750 First Street, NE
Washington, DC 20002
www.apa.org

To order   Tel: (800) 374-2721; Direct: (202) 336-5510
APA Order Department   Fax: (202) 336-5502; TDD/TTY: (202) 336-6123
P.O. Box 92984   Online: www.apa.org/books/
Washington, DC 20090-2984   E-mail: order@apa.org

In the U.K., Europe, Africa, and the Middle East, copies may be ordered from
American Psychological Association
3 Henrietta Street
Covent Garden, London
WC2E 8LU England

Typeset in Minion by World Composition Services, Inc., Sterling, VA

Printer: Edwards Brothers Malloy, Lillington, NC
Cover Designer: Cassandra Chu, San Francisco, CA
Technical/Production Editor: Dan Brachtesende

The opinions and statements published are the responsibility of the author, and such opinions and statements do not necessarily represent the policies of the American Psychological Association.

Library of Congress Cataloging-in-Publication Data

Monastra, Vincent J.
  Parenting children with ADHD : 10 lessons that medicine cannot teach / Vincent J. Monastra.—1st ed.
    p. cm.
  Includes bibliographical references and index.
  ISBN 1-59147-182-6
  ISBN 978-1-59147-182-0
  1. Attention-deficit hyperactivity disorder—Treatment   2. Problem children—Behavior modification.   3. Parenting.   I. Title.

  RJ506.H9M65 2005
  616.85'8906—dc22   2004006147

British Library Cataloguing-in-Publication Data
A CIP record is available from the British Library.

Printed in the United States of America
First Edition

Contents

Parenting
Children
With
ADHD

Introduction

In my early years as a doctor, I found that most of the children I treated responded well to a combination of parental love and thoughtful administration of "consequences" for their actions. However, there was a small, but significant, number of kids who did not. These children would come into my office, week after week. Their parents would tell me about their efforts to get these children to listen, follow rules, remember chores, complete homework, clean their rooms, get along with their brothers and sisters, control their emotions, and develop friendships. Every session would seem the same. Although a child might have been able to improve in some small way, the session invariably turned into a review of his or her greatest "failures" for the week.

Even more torturous were the ensuing discussions in which the child would be asked to provide some explanation for her or his actions. If you have ever tried to have a discussion with a child who has ADHD, you know what I am talking about. Sometimes kids with ADHD will go on and on and on, without ever getting to the point. Sometimes they will be so distracted that you need to repeatedly remind them of the question. Then, just when you're sure they have heard you, you'll get a brief answer like "I don't know," or a shrug. Other times, they will "explode" and storm out of the room before you can get two words out. Even more amazing is the frequency of lying that occurs during discussions. I've witnessed conversations such as one in which a child denied he had broken a family rule and eaten chocolate before dinner, even though his hands and face were smeared with that tasty treat.

My watershed moment came during a 1-week period, approximately 15 years ago. It was the beginning of the summer. I was asked to evaluate two teenage boys. One boy's parents had begun the school year by offering their son the extraordinarily expensive "reward" of a new car, on the basis of his academic performance. The other boy's parents used a typical strategy of "grounding" their son from all social activities, television, and use of electronic games and computers until his grades improved. Which strategy do you think worked? The big bribe? The severe punishment? As it turned out, neither was effective.

Let's take a look at the parents who used the expensive reward. They told their son that if he could complete all his homework, attend all his classes, avoid disciplinary referrals to the principal, and merely "pass" each course for one marking period, they would buy him a new car. He failed to earn the car. After a year of prompting, prodding, encouraging, threatening, yelling, and crying, his parents brought him to me for treatment. Their poignant statement to me was, "something must be seriously wrong with our son."

The other boy's parents took a different approach. In an effort to motivate their son to improve his grades, they restricted his activities. In essence, they told their son that he was "totally grounded": no calls, no contact with his friends after school or on the weekend, no involvement in school activities, no television, and no computer or video games. He was to spend his time completing his school assignments, studying, and resting for the school day. Their deal was simple: Pass all courses for one marking period and you are free. He never did. This boy was grounded for an entire year before he came to my office. I thought the family was kidding. One look at this teen's face told me the sad truth. This was no joke.

Think about the realities of these two stories for a minute. Put yourself in these teens' place. Let's say your mom and dad offered to buy you a new car if you would go to school, stay out of trouble, complete and turn in your homework, and just pass your courses. I don't know about you, but I'd be talking with my folks about make, model, and color scheme for much of the first marking period and would be driving my new car by Thanksgiving. Turn it around. Let's say my folks "totally" grounded me. Once I got over being furious, I would have been determined to stay out of trouble, get my work done, and pass those stupid classes. There is no doubt in my mind that I could have done it. Same is true for you—if you don't have ADHD.

However, if you have ADHD, you, like my two teenage patients, would be bumming rides from friends or trying to sneak in a little television time. You'd continue to fail in school, prompting your parents and teachers to comment that you are unmotivated, have a poor attitude, and "could do better if you tried harder." At home, you would become increasingly distant from your parents, cutting yourself off from two of the most essential sources of love and self-confidence.

This book represents a compilation of the lessons I learned about ways to help children with ADHD succeed. It is an effort to synthesize available medical, nutritional, educational, and psychological research into a format that can be used as a guidebook for parents or health care professionals conducting parenting classes. The book follows the structure of the parenting class provided at my clinic to caregivers after their child has been diagnosed with ADHD.

After conducting these parenting classes for years, I have been struck by the complexity of the available materials and by how difficult it is to use this information in an organized manner. In a similar fashion, I have been aware that a substantial number of my ADHD patients are parented by adults who also have ADHD. As a result, I have tried to write this book as a series of sequential lessons to be taken "one at a time." As I realize that life at home can't come to a standstill until you read the next lesson, I have attempted to incorporate certain "lifelines" that you can use as you progress through this book.

I begin by sharing information about the causes of ADHD. I hope that as you learn about the biological factors that can cause problems of inattention, impulsivity, and hyperactivity in a child, you will eliminate any sense of guilt you may have regarding your role in causing your child's problems. As you come to understand the causes of ADHD, you will learn why the strategies other parents use to raise their children have failed with your child. ADHD is not a medical condition that will magically respond to any specific type of parental correction, nor will it be cured by any of the present forms of medical or psychological treatment.

ADHD is a condition that profoundly affects one's ability to succeed at home, school, work and in social relationships. However, kids with ADHD can develop improved attention, behavioral control, and social skills. Although teachers, physicians, psychologists, and other health care professionals can assist in your efforts to help your child succeed, in the end you will realize that you are your child's best advocate and primary teacher in this process.

Initially, you and your child's physician will need to make sure that other kinds of medical problems are not interfering with your child's ability to listen, learn, and control his or her moods and actions. To help you understand the kinds of medical issues involved,

I review other medical disorders that can cause impairments of attention, mood, and behavioral control. In addition, as part of your consultation with a physician you will probably be asked to consider the range of medical interventions that can reduce the core symptoms of ADHD. Because medication issues are routinely discussed in the treatment of children with ADHD, I review the primary and secondary types of medical treatments to help you understand how these medications affect the underlying causes of ADHD.

In addition to medical treatments, this book emphasizes the importance of other interventions that are needed to help your child. I review information regarding dietary factors and encourage you to examine the adequacy of your child's diet, as certain foods are essential for mental functioning. I present a summary of educational laws and provide information needed to help you work collaboratively with your child's school district. I focus on helping you teach life skills that will help your child succeed on the playground, in school, in the workplace, and one day, as a spouse and parent. I also examine promising psychological treatments for promoting your child's cognitive and social development. Finally, because "parents are people too," I explore ways to create time and space for you to enjoy some pleasurable moments with your child, friends, and loved ones. To help you apply the lessons contained in this book, I have included various worksheets, charts, and checklists. Feel free to photocopy these forms for *your* personal use only.

One last thought before you begin. In my work with parents, I have noted three traits that breed success. First, the parents who report the most progress in their children take it one lesson at a time and do their homework. These parents accept the reality that they will not be able to make headway on all of their children's problems at once. They focus on the goals of a particular lesson and they follow through. Second, my most successful parents remember that lessons learned in one class need to be continued as the course progresses. They usually have a game plan that they review weekly and continue to do so on an ongoing basis. Third, parents whose kids succeed are persistent. If things are not working out the way they hoped, they ask questions, seek clarification, and revise their approach.

You may be wondering, "What's the payoff?" I had that question, too. So I studied the outcomes of children treated at my clinic and looked closely at parenting style. A scientific paper that describes this study in detail was published in the journal, *Applied Psychophysiology and Biofeedback* (see Supplemental Readings for details). First, I made sure that all the children had been thoroughly evaluated for ADHD (and other medical problems) and were being treated with medication for their ADHD. Then, I took the time to work with schools to develop support programs for these children. During this process, parents began our parenting program. At the end of a year, the progress of their children was evaluated. The results indicated that parents who systematically used the lessons taught in this book had children who showed significantly fewer symptoms of ADHD at home. My hope is that you will have similar success with your child.

As you read this book, you may find yourself wanting more detailed information about a particular topic. To help you in your search, I have included a listing of selected books and scientific papers. These supplemental readings are listed by lesson and can be found at the end of the book. With that said, let's get started.

1

Everybody Doesn't Have
a Little Bit of ADHD!

As a typical American, prone to surfing through the channels on my television, I have often witnessed the following scene. Two chairs. Coffee table. Plastic flowers. Books in the background. One reporter. One expert in the studio (the advocate expert). One expert (with an opposing viewpoint) is available via satellite for comment. The topic: ADHD.

Invariably, the "in-studio" expert is asked to define ADHD. This doctor provides some variation of the following statement: "ADHD is a psychiatric disorder that is characterized by symptoms of inattention, with or without evidence of hyperactivity. These symptoms occur prior to 7 years of age. The condition does not disappear with age; it is likely to cause impairment throughout a person's life. Patients diagnosed with ADHD are inattentive, seem to act without thinking, fail to listen to instructions, and have difficulty concentrating at school and completing their schoolwork. These children are at risk to drop out of school and use illegal drugs, and eventually have difficulty succeeding at work and in their marriages." The advocate expert typically proceeds to indicate that ADHD is a "real" medical condition that is inherited and makes reference to a biochemical "imbalance" that causes the disorder.

Next, the opposing side is heard. The expert offers comments that suggest that "everyone has a bit of ADHD." The expert contends that ADHD is a condition that has been dreamed up by pharmaceutical companies and a group of doctors who have conspired to make billions of dollars by selling drugs to kids. Typically, this expert makes some reference to the dangers of promoting addiction in children and excusing them from accepting responsibility for their actions. Sometimes an anthropological spin is presented, which suggests that kids with ADHD are like "hunters" living in a society that no longer needs that type of service. The conclusion of the interview consists of a listing of ADHD symptoms with a recommendation that if your child shows these symptoms, you should consult with his or her physician.

At first glance, that conclusion may sound okay. However, it skirts the real issue. Is ADHD really a medical condition that requires treatment? Or is it just a term used by people to avoid responsibility, or to drug kids and make tons of money? To answer that question, the National Institutes of Health (NIH) organized a meeting in 1998 (NIH Consensus Conference on the Diagnosis and Treatment of ADHD. The complete Consensus Statement is available on the NIH Web site). During this three-day meeting, I and hundreds of other ADHD specialists met in Bethesda, MD, to review the scientific evidence regarding the causes and treatments for ADHD. Because ADHD is one of the most extensively researched "disorders" in our society, the NIH was able to examine the results of over a thousand scientific studies. Based on this review, the NIH concluded that ADHD was indeed a health impairment that (when untreated) increased a person's risk for failure at school, for involvement in substance abuse and criminal activities, and for the development of a variety of problems at work and in social relationships.

ADHD is a condition that is diagnosed based on the presence of a degree of inattention or hyperactivity and impulsivity that is so great that it interferes with a person's ability to succeed at home, school, work, or in relationships with others. Physicians, psychologists, and other qualified health care professionals diagnose ADHD based on the presence of symptoms that are listed in the *Diagnostic and Statistical Manual of Mental Disorders* (DSM–IV; American Psychiatric Association, 1994). In order for a person to be diagnosed with ADHD, he or she must meet five separate standards (called "criteria"). These criteria have to do with the number of symptoms, the age at which these symptoms first caused difficulties, the situations in which these symptoms are shown, and the presence of "impairment" of functioning at school, at work, or in social relationships. In addition, it must be shown that these symptoms are not caused by another mental or physical disorder.

THE FIVE CRITERIA NEEDED TO DIAGNOSE ADHD

The first criterion for a diagnosis of ADHD has to do with the number of symptoms of inattention, hyperactivity, or impulsivity shown by a person. Strange as it may sound, not all patients with ADHD will show symptoms of inattention. Similarly, not all patients with ADHD will be hyperactive, which is kind of confusing. *To be diagnosed with ADHD, the patient must show at least six symptoms of inattention, impulsivity, or hyperactivity. These symptoms must have been observed for at least six months.* If patients only show symptoms of inattention, they meet one of the criteria for the diagnosis of ADHD, Predominately Inattentive Type. If they only show symptoms of hyperactivity–impulsivity, they meet one of the criteria for the diagnosis of ADHD, Predominately Hyperactive–Impulsive Type. If they show both inattention and hyperactivity–impulsivity, they meet the first criteria to be diagnosed with ADHD, Combined Type.

This definition of the subtypes of ADHD can be confusing, so many people use the term *ADD* when a patient only has problems with attention and the term *ADHD* when hyperactivity is a problem. My guess is that these terms will be included in future editions of the diagnostic manual used by doctors. However, this manual currently lists ADHD, Predominately Inattentive Type; ADHD, Predominately Hyperactive–Impulsive Type; and ADHD, Combined Type, as the primary kinds of ADHD. Throughout this book, whenever the term ADHD is used, it refers to patients who present with problems of attention alone, or in combination with symptoms of hyperactivity and impulsivity.

Here is the *DSM–IV's* definition of these terms:

Inattention

There are nine types of inattentive behaviors that are listed in *DSM–IV*. The patient must show the behavior "often" for it to be considered cause for concern. The behaviors are described in the following:

> a. fails to give close attention to details or makes careless mistakes in schoolwork, work, or other activities;
> b. has difficulty sustaining attention in tasks or play activities;
> c. does not seem to listen when spoken to directly;
> d. does not follow through on instructions and fails to finish schoolwork, chores, or duties in the workplace (not because of oppositional behavior or failure to understand instructions);
> e. has difficulty organizing tasks and activities;
> f. avoids, dislikes, or is reluctant to engage in tasks that require sustained mental effort (such as schoolwork or homework);
> g. loses things necessary for tasks or activities (e.g., toys, school assignments, pencils, books, or tools);

h. is easily distracted by extraneous stimuli; and

i. is forgetful in daily activities.

Hyperactivity–Impulsivity

There are six types of hyperactive behaviors and three types of impulsive behaviors that are listed in the diagnostic manual used by physicians and psychologists. As with inattentive behaviors, a person must show at least six of these nine symptoms "often" to meet the first criterion for a diagnosis of ADHD. The specific behaviors are described in the following:

Hyperactivity

a. fidgets with hands or feet or squirms in seat;

b. leaves seat in classroom or in other situations in which remaining seated is expected;

c. runs about or climbs excessively in situations in which it is inappropriate (in adolescents or adults, may be limited to subjective feelings of restlessness);

d. has difficulty playing or engaging in leisure activities quietly;

e. is "on the go" or often acts as if "driven by a motor"; and

f. talks excessively.

Impulsivity

g. blurts out answers before the questions have been completed;

h. has difficulty awaiting turn; and

i. interrupts or intrudes on others (e.g., butts into conversations or games).

Thus, to determine whether your child has ADHD, he or she needs to have at least 6 symptoms of inattention, or 6 of hyperactivity–impulsivity, or a combination of 6 of each (12 total). If that seems true about your child, then she or he meets part of the first criterion for this diagnosis.

An equally important part of this first criterion is that the symptoms of inattention, impulsivity, or hyperactivity occur more frequently than would be expected for the child's age. Because of the need to compare a child's behavior with that of other children, doctors often ask parents, teachers, and others who are familiar with a child to complete "behavioral rating" questionnaires. These forms ask a person to provide information about the kinds of ADHD symptoms they observe and the frequency with which these symptoms occur. If the ratings provided by parents or others indicate that the frequency of a child's inattentive, hyperactive, or impulsive behaviors is greater than at least 93% of their peers, then test results are considered "supportive" of a diagnosis of ADHD. Doctors typically require that a child demonstrate a symptom severity of at least 93% of peers in order to consider diagnosing a patient with any type of illness or condition. Although these rating forms cannot be used as the basis for diagnosis, they provide a useful way to compare a child's behavior with that of other children of the same age.

The second criterion for the diagnosis of ADHD concerns the child's age when symptoms first started to cause problems. *In order for a doctor to diagnose ADHD, at least some ADHD symptoms had to be causing difficulties at home or school before 7 years of age.* This does not mean the child had to be diagnosed with ADHD prior to the age of 7. It just means that evidence of impairment because of inattention, impulsivity, or hyperactivity had to be observed by 7 years of age.

The requirement that symptoms were causing problems at home or school by 7 years of age can cause confusion as parents seek help for their children. Parents often function as a child's "brain" for years, repeatedly reminding the child about responsibilities, helping the child stay organized, endlessly "explaining" family rules, and working for hours on end to help their child keep on top of homework. Consequently, when two parents wonder whether their 12-year-old son (who is not doing his homework and is disrupting the class) has ADHD, eyebrows are raised. After all, isn't a lack of interest in schoolwork a common trait of junior high students? And besides, if the child really did have ADHD, wouldn't it have been diagnosed by 7 years of age?

Over the years, clinical researchers have learned that although some children with ADHD are diagnosed by 7 years of age, most are identified at later ages. In reviewing clinical records, I find several primary periods when children are referred for an evaluation for ADHD. The first occurs between 3 and 5 years of age. These children are quite impulsive and hyperactive. Their parents or guardians are typically

18

terrified about potential injuries that could occur because of their child's behavior, exhausted by the demands of protecting their child, and at a loss to explain why the kinds of discipline that work for everybody else's kids doesn't work for them.

The second period occurs toward the end of the primary grades (about third grade). At this age, I begin to receive referrals to evaluate children who struggle to maintain attention and concentration and who are having difficulties completing school assignments. In addition, hyperactive children who were considered simply immature at 5 or 6 years of age begin to be referred for evaluation because their behavior is severely disruptive in the classroom.

The third period occurs during middle school years. Both inattentive and hyperactive–impulsive children who are failing to succeed in school despite repeated teacher conferences and parental discipline are referred during this time. These children are typically considered unmotivated or emotionally disturbed. "Inattentive" children are suspected of being depressed because they have few friends, engage in little spontaneous conversation, and show little response to rewards or punishments. "Hyperactive–impulsive" children are suspected of having a conduct disorder or an oppositional defiant disorder because they lie, argue with parents, defy parental and school rules, and display frequent outbursts of temper.

The fourth period occurs in high school, when a child has been repeatedly suspended from school and appears at risk to "drop out." These children are rarely referred by a school district. They are usually referred by parents who have seen a television program on ADHD, or who have read a book, magazine article, or story in the paper about ADHD and began to realize that their child had many symptoms of this disorder but was never diagnosed.

These are the kids whose kindergarten teachers had called them exuberant, full of energy, and creative. They had teachers in the primary grades who recognized their intelligence but were concerned because the children had difficulty listening, following directions, concentrating, and completing assignments. By the middle school years, these same children are described as "unmotivated." They are the children who "could do better if they tried harder." They are told that "they should be able to" take notes, read textbooks for essential details, study, and complete their assignments. If tested for learning disabilities, their parents are told they do not qualify for help because they do not have learning disabilities in reading, mathematics, or writing (I examine this issue more fully in lesson 5). These children often misbehave in class, are frequently truant, are disciplined for violating school policies, and are repeatedly punished by their parents.

The final period in which children are referred to me is after high school. Among these patients are children with incredibly committed parents who worked tirelessly to address their children's problems with inattention, disorganization, and failure to complete schoolwork. These young adults commonly report that their parents would devote four to eight hours per day to help them study and complete homework. These patients often had tutors on a daily basis. However, when they began attending college, their problems in attending, note taking, comprehending while reading, writing, and studying surfaced. These students, who were frequently on the honor roll in high school, are typically floundering to pass college level courses, and their parents are at a loss to explain why.

The other group of patients referred after high school are young adults who have developed significant substance abuse or legal problems, yet their parents are convinced that they "are not bad kids." These children have typically dropped out of college, have a pattern of being fired or quitting jobs, have little money, and display highly aggressive and abusive behavior toward their parents. Their parents are likely to have recently "discovered" ADHD and have recognized a pattern of inattention, impulsivity, or hyperactivity that began in early childhood. These parents "hope" that their children have this disorder so they will finally have a diagnosis to explain their children's behaviors.

Because of research published in this area, health care professionals understand that there is no age limit for diagnosing ADHD. The diagnosis is not restricted to early childhood. It does not need to be made during grade school or even by the conclusion of high school. The condition can persist and interfere with a person's success throughout his or her life. *Consequently*, regardless of your child's age, if some ADHD symptoms were causing problems at home or at school by 7 years of age, the child meets the second criterion for a diagnosis of ADHD.

The third criterion for ADHD requires that "some" impairment from the symptoms is present in two or more settings (e.g., home, school, work, or social relationships). This does not mean that the results of behavioral rating scales *have to* show that the frequency of symptoms is greater than at least 93% of peers at home and at school. It means that evidence of ADHD symptoms needs to be observed in more than one setting and that these symptoms have to interfere with a child's success in these settings. Thus, if a child is experiencing parental anger (instead of praise and acceptance) because she or he is careless, fails to attend, does not listen, is disorganized, avoids homework, and so on, then these symptoms are causing impairment at home. Similarly, if the child is being prevented from playing at recess; is being detained after school to complete schoolwork; is being scolded, belittled, or reprimanded; is being removed from class; or is receiving failing grades because of ADHD symptoms, then his or her symptoms are causing impairment at school. If these types of problems are occurring with your child, then your child meets the third criterion for a diagnosis of ADHD.

The fourth criterion for ADHD requires that there must be "clear evidence of clinically significant impairment in social, academic or occupational functioning." What is "clear evidence"? Certainly, the presence of failing grades in school qualifies if the child has at least average intelligence. In addition, depending on grade expectations, if a child is unable to record homework assignments, bring home necessary materials, take notes in class, read textbooks for detail and understanding, complete written assignments, prepare study guides, and study for tests because of attentional problems, these too can be considered a sign of impairment. So can a child's lack of friends, difficulties in resolving peer conflicts, or an inability to engage in meaningful conversations. Chances are that if you are a parent reading this book, your child is likely to be struggling to pass class requirements at school and lacks friends. If so, your child meets the fourth criterion for ADHD.

In my opinion, the final criterion for ADHD is often ignored or minimized by health care professionals. *It requires that the doctor diagnosing ADHD ensures that the symptoms of inattention, impulsivity, or hyperactivity are not caused by another mental or physical disorder.* We live in an era in which the need for laboratory tests is closely scrutinized, and there is a tendency to question the need for blood tests or other diagnostic procedures prior to determining a diagnosis of ADHD. I have real concerns about restrictions on diagnostic tests and strongly recommend that patients receive a thorough evaluation for all medical conditions that can be contributing to their attentional problems. Here's why.

Do you know that symptoms of inattention are a characteristic of hypoglycemia? Of anemia? Of diabetes? Of thyroid disorders? Of sleep apnea? Of allergies? Of dietary insufficiencies of zinc and magnesium? Are you aware that concentration problems while reading or writing could be associated with difficulties in visual tracking and convergence that are not easily detected in a routine examination of visual acuity? Maybe you are, but maybe you aren't. If you aren't aware that problems of attention, hyperactivity, and impulsivity can be caused by medical problems other than ADHD, then a review of any standard medical text (e.g., Cecil's Textbook of Medicine) or a medical search using WebMD (or other reputable Web site) could be enlightening.

Your doctor is, or should be, aware that the conditions listed above (and others) can cause symptoms of inattention, impulsivity, and hyperactivity. Although I have participated in the evaluation and treatment of over 10,000 patients with significant problems in attention or behavioral control, I have rarely encountered a patient who had been screened for these conditions prior to seeing me. In fact, it is not uncommon for a physician to inform me that she or he did not screen for these conditions because there was no medical reason to do so. I respectfully disagree. Because patients suspected of ADHD have a significant problem attending, and patients with each of these other medical problems also have significant attentional problems, I think there is sufficient cause to evaluate a patient for other medical problems. So does the *DSM–IV*.

The guidelines established by the American Psychiatric Association require that a physician, psychologist, or other health care provider makes sure that another medical condition is not causing the ADHD symptoms. Tests for these conditions are reliable, relatively inexpensive, and readily available; I advocate their use. During presentations to physicians and psychologists, I ask how they would feel if they discovered that a patient they treated for ADHD actually had sleep apnea, hypoglycemia, a thyroid disorder, or another medical condition? As parents and guardians, I have to ask you the same question. Once you are assured that your child's symptoms are not attributable to another medical problem, you are ready for the next step.

HOMEWORK

Prior to reading the next lesson, take a little time to digest this information. In this lesson, I gave you a summary of the components required for a diagnosis of ADHD. If you suspect that your child meets these criteria but has not been evaluated for ADHD or the other medical conditions that can cause such symptoms, make arrangements to have such an evaluation completed. Similarly, if your child has been diagnosed with ADHD but has not been evaluated for other medical conditions that could cause its symptoms, I encourage you to obtain this medical evaluation. It may represent a slight inconvenience for you and your child. However, if your child happens to be among the 4% of patients who have other medical causes for their ADHD symptoms, it may be the smartest move you ever make.

2

Parenting Doesn't Cause ADHD, Genes Do!

As noted in lesson 1, there has been much public debate about the causes of ADHD. Some Americans believe that ADHD is a fictional condition, created by pharmaceutical companies and doctors to drum up business. Others consider it a condition caused by parents who spoil their children. Still others note the reactions of children to certain foods (e.g., wheat or corn), food dyes, or preservatives and argue that dietary habits are responsible for ADHD.

The scientific evidence available at this time indicates that none of the above is true; however, like any type of opinion, there is a bit of truth underlying each of these positions. Corporate greed can be a problem in any business endeavor. "Spoiling" does not help the development of any child, but there is no evidence that parenting style causes ADHD. Similarly, although certain children do display symptoms of inattention, impulsivity, or hyperactivity because of allergies (or other medical problems), ADHD is a distinct medical condition that by definition is not caused by other medical or psychiatric disorders.

As I indicated in lesson 1, ADHD is not diagnosed simply by the presence of inattention, impulsivity, or hyperactivity. Because various medical conditions can cause such symptoms, the diagnosis also requires medical testing to rule out the presence of other health problems whose symptoms mimic ADHD. For example, patients with diabetes can routinely experience difficulties in concentrating if they ignore dietary recommendations or fail to follow their physicians' orders regarding the use of medication. Doctors don't call their condition "ADHD." Patients who have anemia can be forgetful, easily fatigued, unable to concentrate and attend to task, and can become disorganized and irritable. Again, doctors don't say that a person with anemia "has ADHD." This is also the case for individuals with other medical conditions such as hypoglycemia, thyroid disorders, certain types of allergies, sleep disorders, and dietary insufficiencies of zinc and magnesium. Such symptoms can also be noted in children who have visual problems, hearing loss, and specific learning disabilities (e.g., reading, mathematics, and written expression). Because there are multiple medical pathways that can lead to symptoms of inattention, hyperactivity, or impulsivity, the mere presence of these symptoms does not mean that a person has ADHD.

The diagnosis of ADHD requires that doctors conduct thorough evaluations of patients to determine what is causing these symptoms. If a patient has at least six symptoms of inattention or hyperactivity–impulsivity and these symptoms have been present since at least 7 years of age, have been observed in at least two settings (e.g., home, school, community), are causing significant functional problems in at least one of these settings, and are not due to any other medical condition, then a diagnosis of ADHD can be determined. However, knowing this does not help us really understand why 5%–10% of American children have problems attending, concentrating, and controlling their actions despite the efforts of their parents and teachers.

So, What Is ADHD?

ADHD is a psychiatric condition that has been primarily associated with a pattern of excessive inactivity in the frontal lobes of the brain. This basically means that the part of a person's body that is in charge of thinking, planning, concentrating, and "staying on task" is not as active as it needs to be in order for a person to succeed at school, at work, and at home. When children, teens, and adults with ADHD have been examined with a variety of brain imaging techniques (e.g., PET scans, SPECT scans, or Quantitative EEGs), a pattern of "underarousal" has been evident in the vast majority of these patients.

Beginning in the early 1990s, published scientific reports have revealed that patients with ADHD show a slowing in the rate that glucose (sugar) is used in the frontal lobes. We also have learned that a slowing of oxygen flow into the frontal lobes typically occurs in patients with ADHD. Finally, when the electrical "output" of brain cells is examined in these patients, this same pattern of slowing is noted in the electrical activity recorded from brain cells in this region.

What Causes This "Inactivity" in the Brain?

The application of neuroimaging technology has greatly increased understanding of how underarousal of the brain may occur. Scientists have long known that brain cells communicate by releasing certain chemicals called neurotransmitters. In order for a message to be sent and received by other cells, a bit of neurotransmitter must be released, avoid being reabsorbed by a reuptake transport system (that attempts to bring released neurotransmitters back into the cell), travel across a space between cells called a "synapse," and activate docking stations or receptors on the nearby brain cells. If sufficient activation of the nearby cell occurs, then that cell releases neurotransmitters and the process of communication continues.

Take a few minutes to look at the illustration in Figure 2.1. You'll notice that the picture of the brain highlights the frontal lobe (particularly the prefrontal cortex). This is the region of the brain that is important for attention and concentration. When it is activated, your child is able to block out distractions and create

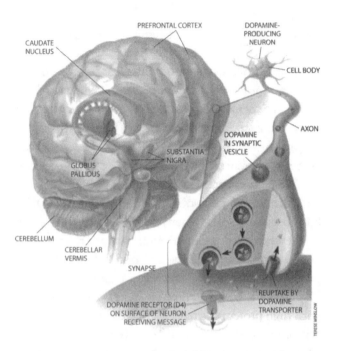

FIGURE 2.1. Brain structures essential for attention and concentration. Copyright 1998 by Terese Winslow. Reprinted with permission.

enough mental energy to concentrate on one task at a time. On the other hand, when this region is not sufficiently activated, the child will be unable to focus on your instructions, understand what he or she is reading, or "think" before acting.

The way that brain cells communicate is illustrated by the adjacent picture of a single "transmitting" cell and a nearby receiving cell. The transmitter cell is releasing small amounts of neruotransmitter into the space between the two cells (synapse). You can see particles of neurotransmitter attaching to the dopamine receptor and other particles being reabsorbed. The brain chemicals that attach to dopamine receptors cause the awakening of the brain. Those neurotransmitters that are reabsorbed by the dopamine transporter get returned to the transmitting cell for later use.

While there are numerous types of neurotransmitters, the one of primary interest in studies of ADHD has been dopamine. Dopamine is found in the regions of the brain that are involved in attention, thinking, and control of our moods and our movements. It is produced in the ventral tegmental region of the brain. Dopamine is manufactured in our bodies from foods with high protein content, such as meats, fish, poultry, eggs, dairy products, certain beans (e.g., soy), and nuts. This manufacturing process takes place primarily in the morning and early afternoon. Although the body is capable of storing a certain amount of dopamine, the truth is that if we fail to eat a breakfast that includes a sufficient amount of protein, we will have difficulty concentrating by mid-morning whether we have ADHD or not. If the first time during the day that a person eats protein is at lunch, it is likely that he or she will feel quite sluggish and inattentive within an hour of lunchtime.

Because of the connection between dietary protein and attention, one of the aspects of treatment that I emphasize is finding a way to get at least 15–20 grams of protein into a patient's breakfast and lunch. I review strategies for improving nutrition in lesson 4. However, it is important to realize that consuming a sufficient amount of protein will not "cure" ADHD. What it will do is make it possible for a patient's brain cells to have an adequate supply of dopamine (and other neurotransmitters) to "communicate" with other brain cells.

We have learned that ADHD is not caused by an insufficient amount of stored dopamine. Instead, the problem appears to be related to what happens when a brain cell tries to release dopamine to "talk" to other brain cells. There is evidence that patients with ADHD have a reuptake system that reabsorbs about 70% more of the released dopamine than people who don't have ADHD. That means the brain cells of patients with ADHD are transmitting far less neuro-transmitter to nearby cells than people who don't have ADHD. In addition, there is evidence that the brain cells that are receiving dopamine have approximately 16% fewer "docking" sites (called receptors). The result is that nearby cells are not being activated as quickly. This underactivity is what is evident on QEEG scans, PET scans, and SPECT scans. Current scientific evidence suggests that this underactivity is what causes patients with ADHD to have difficulty sustaining attention, concentrating, thinking, regulating their emotional responses, and controlling their behavior.

Do All Children With ADHD Show Underarousal of the Frontal Lobes?

No. A series of recent scientific studies using SPECT and QEEG procedures have revealed that approximately 10%–15% of patients with ADHD do not show such patterns. Interestingly, this research has also suggested that this type of patient tends to respond poorly to stimulant medications. It is unclear whether patients in this "subgroup" of ADHD (who demonstrate excessive activity over frontal regions) actually have ADHD, or if they have another type of neurological disorder that is characterized by symptoms of inattention, impulsivity, and hyperactivity.

How Did My Child Get This Condition?

Although children who experience prenatal exposure to alcohol, heroin or cocaine, birth trauma, or lead poisoning are likely to have attentional and other neurodevelopmental problems, I consider it confusing to diagnose such children with ADHD. Similarly, I think it is confusing to use the term ADHD if attentional and behavioral problems are shown by patients with diabetes, hypoglycemia, thyroid disorders, anemia, allergies, sleep apnea, and other medical conditions. Only if the ADHD symptoms persisted after these medical conditions were adequately treated would I consider a diagnosis of ADHD to be appropriate.

The current understanding of ADHD is that it is an inherited condition. ADHD occurs in approximately 3%–10% of the American population. However, that rate increases dramatically in families where there is at least one parent who also has this disorder. About 57% of adults with ADHD will have at least one child with this condition. If you have a child who has been diagnosed with ADHD, the chance that another of your children will have ADHD increases to about 33%.

What is Inherited?

Two primary types of inherited traits have been investigated. The evidence to date indicates that patients with ADHD are likely to demonstrate atypical genetic characteristics on chromosomes that are responsible for creating dopamine transporters and dopamine receptors. That is what is believed to cause the "underarousal" of the brain. While there are some inconsistencies in which specific receptor type is responsible for the problem (there are six), the high rate of inheritability of ADHD is not an issue of debate at this time.

What Does All This Mean?

ADHD is an inherited, medical condition that appears to be primarily caused by an underarousal of the regions of the brain that regulate mood, control behavior, and help one pay attention. This underarousal seems to be related to a problem in brain cells that use dopamine to communicate. Patients with ADHD appear to have dopamine pathways that allow too much dopamine to be reabsorbed, with an insufficient amount of dopamine transmitted or received by nearby cells. As a result, effective treatments need to target this underlying problem to achieve significant improvement.

Why Use Medicines to Treat ADHD?

Medicines for ADHD represent the most common type of treatment for this condition. Typically, patients with ADHD are treated with stimulant medications (e.g., Ritalin or the generic form, methylphenidate). More recently, non-stimulant medications for ADHD symptoms also have been developed (e.g., Strattera). ADHD medications can be used alone or in combination with other medicines that reduce excessive anger, anxiety, or depression (e.g., Zoloft, Paxil, Depakote, Catapres, and Tenex).

ADHD medicines work in several ways. Some block the action of the "dopamine reuptake system" (e.g., methylphenidate, Ritalin, Concerta, and Metadate), which allows more dopamine to activate nearby brain cells. Other medications (e.g., Dexedrine) stimulate the release of dopamine, resulting in increased levels of this neurotransmitter at receptor sites. A third type of stimulant (Adderall) achieves a combination of these effects and also enhances the action of norepinephrine (another neurotransmitter). Non-stimulant ADHD medications, such as Strattera, primarily block the action of the norepinephrine reuptake system, which enhances the transmission of neural pathways that use this neurotransmitter. If a patient is consuming an adequate amount of dietary protein, these medications are typically well tolerated. However, the efficacy among patients who do not eat protein at breakfast and lunch appears to be reduced and the frequency of side effects (e.g., headache, insomnia, stomachache, irritability) is increased.

PSYCHOLOGICAL AND EDUCATIONAL TREATMENTS FOR ADHD

Research has indicated that patients with ADHD are more successful at home, school, and in the community if their treatment includes a combination of medication and other types of interventions. Several types of treatment have been shown to yield positive results in both case studies and controlled group studies. These include the following:

- the development of a program of academic support and accommodation at school;
- parenting classes to teach strategies that systematically use reinforcement to help children and adolescents develop essential life skills;
- social skills classes that help kids learn how to start and maintain conversations, establish friendships and resolve conflicts, and build self-confidence;
- EEG biofeedback (sometimes called neurotherapy), which promotes the development of attention and behavioral control by helping patients

learn how to regulate the level of "arousal" in the regions of the brain that control these functions;
- individual and family therapy to address problems of trauma, inadequate parental nurturance, and excessive conflict in the home.

Although I take a little time to describe each of these treatments, this book does not concentrate on how others can help your child. The purpose of this book is to help *you* learn ways to promote your child's success. The lessons to be shared involve learning about medication, nutrition, the educational rights of your child, and parenting approaches that can help your child mature. While your parenting style did not cause ADHD, there is much that you can do to help.

HOMEWORK

There are numerous concerns that parents have when it comes to their child's development. This week, I'd like you to look at the list of lessons that you might want your child to learn (found at the end of this lesson). Check off those that you'd like to teach your child. As we work together to help your child develop skills, we'll use this as a reference. Try not to get discouraged if you find yourself checking off 30 or 40 problems. Later in this book, I'll suggest that you focus on about a half dozen of your most pressing concerns, just to help you get comfortable. Once the techniques described in this book become part of your family life, it is a lot easier to address other problem areas.

After you pick out the lessons that you want to teach, I'd like you to consider establishing the "Parent–Child Non-Aggression Pact."

The Parent–Child Non-Aggression Pact

Change is not readily accepted in any organization, and families that include a patient diagnosed with ADHD are no exception. In addition, children and teens with ADHD are highly reactive to change in their environment and are likely to become verbally or physically aggressive when they don't get their way. To set the stage for teaching lessons, it helps to establish a "Parent–Child Non-Aggression Pact." The first part of this family rule is simply this: *"It is not okay for anyone in the family to yell, threaten, hit, tease, or be mean to another family member."* That is not to say it won't happen. Let's face it, at times you'll get angry and your child will get angry. Most likely, there will be moments when mean words are spoken. When that happens, I'd like you to consider instituting the second part of the "Parent–Child Non-Aggression Pact": *"If a family member says or does something that is hurtful, when they cool off, they will apologize and do something to make up."* That goes for everyone.

In life, when we do (or say) something to another person that is hurtful, we owe that person an apology. It's also a good idea to try to make "amends." I want my patients to learn that their parents are people and that it is important to be sensitive to the needs and feelings of others. So, if they yell at their parents for 15 minutes, stomp around the living room, and slam doors just because they had to stop playing X-Box, that is not okay. *Before they can resume playing anything,* they will need to apologize and do something to "make amends" (e.g., do an extra chore; write a note describing what they should do instead of yelling; list why mom or dad deserves to be respected; write a note describing what they like about mom or dad; make a snack for the family). I often say to my patients that if you make someone's life harder, you need to apologize and do something to make it better. So before you begin the next lesson, pick a calm moment, sit down with your children, explain this new family rule, and try it out.

When I offer this suggestion in my parenting classes, I have often heard parents wonder why I wouldn't encourage them to simply "ground" the child from use of their video game system for a day or a week, instead of this "make-up" stuff. Certainly, that makes sense for a lot of kids. However, children with ADHD tend to either "blow up" further when you do "take-aways" or sneak behind your back and play with the forbidden item anyway (hey, you're not there all the time). Now I realize that you could hide the game, disconnect the electricity, and create an armed camp in your home. But to be honest, your child is probably going to relish that battle.

Despite such problems, I have no doubt that an energetic, determined, and forceful parent could pull off such "take-away" strategies. However, as I explain to parents, I'm thinking of the long term. I'd like your child to develop the habit of offering an apology and attempting to "make it up" as early in life as possible. In healthy relationships, we don't take something away from our friend or partner if they upset us or we upset them. Not if we want an enduring relationship. Instead, we offer an apology and attempt to make up. Why not teach that to your child?

WHAT I'D LIKE MY CHILD TO LEARN: DR. MONASTRA'S TOP 40

1. _____ wake up in the morning without battling with me
2. _____ get dressed in clean clothes in the morning
3. _____ eat breakfast that includes some kind of protein (e.g., eggs, meat, soy)
4. _____ take medication
5. _____ brush teeth; wash up; comb hair
6. _____ make bed; pick up room
7. _____ pack school bag with books, homework, etc.
8. _____ not argue with me or brothers or sisters in the morning
9. _____ get to the school bus on time
10. _____ get to classes on time
11. _____ remember to bring the necessary books and materials to class
12. _____ remember to turn in homework
13. _____ sit in seat at school
14. _____ do school work in class
15. _____ speak when called on in class
16. _____ not interrupt the teacher
17. _____ eat a healthy lunch
18. _____ copy down homework assignments
19. _____ remember to bring home the books and materials needed for homework
20. _____ learn how to have conversations with other kids
21. _____ learn how to play and solve disagreements without getting into fights
22. _____ come home after school
23. _____ do homework
24. _____ organize books and school materials so that work doesn't get lost

25. _____ listen and obey parental instructions
26. _____ come home for dinner
27. _____ eat a dinner that includes protein, fruit, and vegetables (in addition to the ever popular pizza, pasta, fries)
28. _____ do chores with minimal prompting
29. _____ play cooperatively with siblings and neighborhood kids
30. _____ put away toys, papers, etc.
31. _____ make bed; clean room
32. _____ not argue with parents
33. _____ learn to solve problems by negotiating
34. _____ spend some time reading, painting, building, practicing word processing skills, or engage in any activity that requires thinking
35. _____ express ideas or feelings without using obscene or vulgar language
36. _____ wash up; brush teeth in the evening
37. _____ go to the bedroom at bedtime and rest quietly
38. _____ stay in the bedroom and let me sleep until morning
39. _____ apologize, accept responsibility for mistakes, and make an effort to make up
40. _____ do something "thoughtful" for another person

Other lessons?

_____

_____

_____

_____

3

Medicines Don't Cure ADHD, but They Can Help

One of the most hotly debated topics in America centers on the use of medications in treating childhood psychiatric disorders like ADHD. At one extreme are advocates of medication who assert that these medicines are effective and absolutely safe for children. These individuals point to the decades of use of stimulant therapy, to "double-blind" studies that show short-term improvement of attention and reduction of hyperactivity and impulsivity, and to the absence of any medical evidence that shows that the use of these medications causes any harm to patients. The poster child for this advocacy group is the kid who was inattentive, out of control, and flunking out of school prior to using medication. After using medication, this same child is maintaining a degree of organization that would make Martha Stewart proud and is a straight "A" student.

At the other extreme are parents and health care professionals who are alarmed that doctors are prescribing stimulant medications to children and teens. These individuals express concern about increasing the risk for substance abuse in children with ADHD, cite evidence that suggests that chronic use of amphetamines may alter brain structures, and consider ADHD to be a condition created by doctors and drug companies to make money and make energetic kids more manageable for lazy parents. The poster child for this advocacy group is the child who became a "zombie" or reacted with increased aggression or hyperactivity to stimulant use.

So ... Who's Telling the Truth?

From my perspective . . . both. One thing I've learned as a doctor is to listen to my patients. As a psychologist who has participated in the evaluation and treatment of over 10,000 patients diagnosed with ADHD and other behavioral disorders, I have seen the poster children from both advocacy groups. There is substantial evidence from research studies and clinical practice that medications for ADHD can improve attention and behavioral control. They also can be used to help patients learn to control commonly occurring emotional problems such as anxiety, depressed mood, and outbursts of temper. If a patient is diagnosed on the basis of a thorough evaluation process, receives a dose of medication that has been properly adjusted, and is eating something more substantial than cereal for breakfast and chips and soda for lunch, then medications like Ritalin-LA, Adderall-XR, Concerta, Metadate-CD and non-stimulant ADHD medications (Strattera) can be helpful.

However, if the diagnosis is based on a cursory interview or a knee jerk reaction to parent or teacher complaints, if dosage is based on age or body weight, and if no attention is paid to a child's dietary patterns, these medications can cause significant short-term problems. I have seen numerous little kids in my office who were responding poorly to stimulants. The typical parent story goes something like this:

"Timmy has been having a hard time sitting still in school ever since kindergarten. His teacher thought that he was just an energetic, bright student and understood that he needed to be able to move around in class. Things went okay that year, but this year his teacher insisted that he stay in his chair and do his class work. Timmy kept getting up and talking with other kids and got angry when his teacher told him to sit down. One day, it got really bad and he pushed his chair at his teacher. She called us and told us that she thought maybe he had ADHD.

So, we took Timmy to see his pediatrician. The doctor spoke with us for 10 minutes and asked us to complete a form that asked a lot of questions about our son's ability to listen, follow directions, and things like that. The doctor also asked us to give the teacher a form for her to fill out. After the forms were completed, we saw the doctor again and were told that Timmy had ADHD. The doctor spoke with us about stimulant medications and we decided to try a type of "Ritalin" that lasted all day. Because our son was only seven, the doctor suggested that we start with Concerta (18 mg).

The first day, Timmy wasn't hungry for breakfast, which wasn't unusual. But we gave him the medication. He went off to school and his teacher told us that she thought he had a pretty good day. He stayed in his seat, seemed to pay attention, and didn't get angry. Timmy complained that his stomach felt upset a little and his head hurt, but this went away. But he didn't eat much lunch, either. That night, Timmy was off the wall. He ran around in circles, yelling and screaming, and wore himself out by 9:00 p.m.

Next day, we still couldn't get any breakfast in Timmy. He took his medication and went to school. That day wasn't as good as the day before, but still his teacher said she thought the medication was helping. After school, we couldn't see any improvement and as the night wore on, Timmy revved up. We decided to call the pediatrician.

The doctor told us that this was common. He suggested that we increase his dose (Concerta, 36 mg). We did. The next day, his teacher told us he was refusing to do his school work. We told Timmy that he couldn't go outside to play. He blew up and trashed his room. Later on, he calmed down a little bit, but that night he didn't fall asleep until 11:00 p.m. I didn't know what to do. I called his doctor the next day.

The doctor told me that some kids start to adjust to their medication after a little while. I was told to keep him on that dose for the rest of the month and to come in for an appointment. That month was hell. My son ate like a bird, was fighting with me and my husband all the time, and refused to do anything at school. When we saw the doctor, we decided to increase his medication to 54 mg of Concerta.

Not much changed for the better after that. Timmy still wouldn't eat, was moody and angry, and got into trouble at school nearly every day. At the end of the month, his doctor said that perhaps we should try a different stimulant. We changed to Adderall-XR (20 mg). Still no change. His doctor said that maybe something else was wrong with Timmy. He suggested that we consult with a psychiatrist or psychologist. We decided to see you, since you specialize in treating kids with ADHD."

So, what went wrong? There are several possibilities. First, Timmy's doctor did not test to see if there was any other medical explanation for his symptoms. In addition, there was no evaluation of the adequacy of his diet and no examination of sleeping patterns. Although I reviewed the importance of diet, adequate sleep, and a thorough medical evaluation in lesson two, these factors cannot be overemphasized if you want your child to succeed.

There is one other explanation for Timmy's poor response to medication: The presence of another neurological condition that is causing his symptoms. During the past 15 years, several research teams have examined thousands of patients with ADHD and found that although the vast majority (80%–90%) demonstrate underactivity in the frontal lobes of the brain, there is a "neurophysiological subgroup" of ADHD patients who do not show such cortical slowing.

Initially this subgroup of ADHD patients was identified by Dr. Daniel Amen with SPECT imaging. Unlike other patients with ADHD, this group demonstrated excessive activity, particularly in a region called the cingulate gyrus. In his treatment of these patients, he has learned that stimulant medications rarely are helpful and has described useful strategies in various books and professional publications. You can find information about his treatment through an Internet search (Amen Clinics; OneADDPlace).

Other research teams using Quantitative EEG procedures also have found evidence of excessive activity in a small but significant number of patients with ADHD (again, about 10%–20%). By measuring the electrical activity of children and teens as they perform academic tasks, our clinic (and other clinical research teams) has demonstrated that those children who do not respond to stimulant medications often do not demonstrate underactivity of the brain. This makes a lot of sense given what we know about response to medication among patients with ADHD.

For example, we know that a substantial percentage of patients with ADHD (15%–30%) will either not respond to stimulant medication or will be unable to tolerate side effects. When such patients have been examined with QEEG, it is frequently found that they do not demonstrate cortical slowing. Consequently, it is not surprising that they would not respond to medications designed to stimulate brain activity. After all, if a patient's brain is not "working too slowly," then why should we expect a stimulant medication to help?

Because of this research, one of the tests I routinely conduct on patients with ADHD is a QEEG examination. I have found that this is particularly helpful in situations in which the child has responded poorly to stimulant medications or if there is skepticism about the medical "reality" of the child's attentional problems. The results of a QEEG examination can help children, parents, and teachers understand the physical nature of ADHD and also can reduce the risk that your child will have a poor response to medication. If you happen to live in an area where this type of QEEG exam is available, I suggest that you consider including it in your child's evaluation. The Association for Applied Psychophysiology and Biofeedback (phone: 303-422-8436) or the International Society for Neuronal Regulation (phone: 800-488-3867) can provide a listing of providers in your region who are qualified to complete such an evaluation.

DO ALL KIDS NEED STIMULANTS?

No. One thing that I want to cover in this lesson is the different types of medications used to treat patients with ADHD. Depending on the kinds of symptoms, some children will be treated with stimulants, some with "non-stimulant" ADHD medications (Strattera), some with antidepressants, some with antihypertensives, and some who will respond well to paired combinations of these medications (e.g., Zoloft, Lexapro,

Catapres, or Tenex with a sustained-release stimulant).
I'll spend the rest of this lesson describing how each
can be helpful in promoting your child's success.

Medicines for Problems of Inattention, Hyperactivity, and Impulsivity

The primary type of treatment for the core symptoms
of ADHD (inattention, hyperactivity, and impulsivity)
is stimulants. As I described in lesson 2, these medications help to increase the activity of brain cells by
either causing more dopamine to be released or interfering with the dopamine reuptake transporter system.
When a person takes a medication like dexedrine,
brain cells that communicate by releasing dopamine
are "stimulated" to increase their activity. Presumably,
the increased availability of dopamine serves to help
the communication between nerve cells responsible
for attention and behavioral control.

In a similar manner, other medications like Ritalin, methylphenidate, and Concerta or Metadate-
CD (more recently developed "time-released" versions
of Ritalin) try to boost the communication of dopamine-bearing brain cells by occupying the dopamine
reuptake transport system. When brain cells release a
bit of their neurotransmitter, the dopamine reuptake
transport system tries to recapture some of this "juice"
so that the cell can send another message. Medicines
like Ritalin (and related compounds) attach to these
reuptake transporters, preventing them from "captur-

ing" dopamine. In doing so, dopamine remains in the space between brain cells (called a synapse) and can activate nearby brain cells. In the case of dopamine-bearing brain cells, the result can be improved attention, concentration, and behavioral control.

The last type of stimulant medication commonly available is called Adderall (or Adderall-XR). This medication is approximately twice as potent as Ritalin. That means 5 mg of Adderall has about the same effect as a 10 mg dose of Ritalin. The reason for this is the dual action of Adderall. Like dexedrine, this medication increases the release of dopamine from brain cells. In addition, like Ritalin, this medication blocks the ability of the dopamine reuptake transport system to re-absorb dopamine after it has been released from a brain cell.

So when your child begins to take a stimulant, your doctor is attempting to treat his or her medical condition by increasing the level of dopamine that is available to be used for communication between brain cells. This increased dopamine activity occurs in regions of the brain responsible for attention and concentration (generally the frontal lobes), in brain structures involved in mood regulation (primarily the thalamus and limbic system), and in neurological centers responsible for "social judgment" and movement (the Cerebellum and the Rolandic cortex). Although dopamine-bearing nerve cells do not carry out these jobs alone (there are numerous other brain chemicals that can be involved), medications that target dopaminergic nerve cells can have a profound effect in improving a child's attention and behavior.

Start-Up Strategies

A strategy that my clinic (and others) has used for identifying the most helpful dose of medication involves collaboration among the child's physician, parents, teachers, and psychologist or psychiatrist. Typically, I encourage a clinical trial of the lowest dose of medication; for example, 18 mg of Concerta, 20 mg of Metadate-CD, or the equivalent of this in other stimulants (e.g., 5 mg of Adderall-XR). I ask parents to complete a Medication Tolerance Checklist to make sure the child is tolerating the medication well. In addition, at my clinic I will test a child's attention using a computerized test of attention (e.g., The Test of Variables of Attention). I have found that children using an optimal dose of medication will score as well as peers without ADHD on these tests when their dose is "correct." I also request that parents and teachers complete a weekly behavioral rating scale to track symptoms at home and school and use hourly checklists (medication response charts) at school if medication effects are wearing out. (Samples of the Medication Tolerance Checklist and Medication Response Chart can be found at the end of this lesson.)

These questionnaires are important for adjusting the amount of medication needed. For example, although medications are supposed to last a certain amount of time, a child's actual response may be quite different. I have worked with children who are using Concerta (a medication that can provide sympto-matic relief for 10–12 hours), yet show poor atten-tion and become hyperactive after 6 hours. Similarly, I have seen children who are being treated with Adderall-XR (which can provide 10–12 hours of clini-cal improvement) show problems with attention, be-havioral control, or moodiness in the late afternoon or early evening. If your child is taking one of these medications but her or his teacher is saying it isn't working, try to track down when the medicine seems to be wearing off.

Sometimes, the need is not for a higher dose. At times, what is needed is a combination with other medications (e.g., antihypertensives like Catapres or Tenex or a "non-stimulant" ADHD medication like Strattera), which can help to reduce hyperactivity and moodiness after school without causing disruption of eating or sleeping habits. At other times a child can show problems at school, not because of the ineffec-tiveness of medication, but because of an underlying learning disorder or because they are being asked to complete tasks (e.g., writing, repetitive copying, or note-taking tasks) that are commonly difficult for chil-dren with ADHD. In those instances, provision of support by a teacher or aide, or permission to use word processing tools (e.g., computer word processing programs or use of dedicated word processors like an Alpha-Smart or Dream Writer) can be helpful.

The deterioration of medication effects is not limited to the school day. However, it sometimes surprises me that parents get the impression that they should just "tough it out" once their children get home. I consider success at home to be just as important for a child's development as success at school. If a child goes home every day and begins to get yelled at, ignored, criticized, hit, grounded, or punished by having their favorite activities taken away from them because they don't listen, play quietly, not interrupt, etc., then the child is not going to be feeling "loved" and cared about. Rather, the child is going to be feeling and acting miserably (and so will you).

Because of this, I also track how the child is doing after school. I consider medication to be somewhat like a knee brace used after a joint injury. It doesn't cure the medical problem, but it helps a person get around and live their life. As I'm one of those weekend warriors with chronic knee and ankle injuries, but who still considers himself to be a bit of an athlete, I need to be careful. If I'm going to be physically active in the morning, I need to tape and use a brace. If I'm going to be physically active in the afternoon, I need to tape and use a brace. And guess what? If I'm playing softball after work, I need to tape and use a brace. If I don't, then my knee is going to collapse and that's not fun. So if I'm a kid who needs medication to help me pay attention, concentrate, and control my reactions to frustration during the day, then the odds are that I'll need to be treated with some type of medication that can help me succeed after school and in the evening.

I often hear that parents and physicians are reluctant to prescribe medications that will remain clinically active in the afternoon and early evening, because of concerns about sleeping problems. It is well known that kids who use stimulants can have a hard time getting to sleep at night. As a result, parents and physicians have been reluctant to prescribe stimulant medication that can help in the late afternoon and early evening. While I respect this caution, I think there are other interventions that can be used, rather than taking a child's medication away for the last four waking hours.

Because I do not ignore the importance of dietary issues at my clinic, I often ask about what a child is eating in the evening. It is far from uncommon to find that a child who can't fall asleep eats very little protein during the day, consumes high-sugar juices and sodas after school and in the evening, and loves to snack on all sorts of energizing carbohydrates (chips, cookies, etc.) and caffeinated foods (e.g., colas and chocolate) in the evening. Consequently, I try to help parents find ways to improve their child's diet (more on that in the next lesson) to reduce adverse effects caused by "stimulatory" foods. This way, the late afternoon and early evening hours can be more successful for you and your child.

How Do I Know That the Dose is the Right One?

The process for determining what type and dose of medication is needed is not a matter of simply starting a medication, asking parents and teachers if it is generally working, and then increasing dose or changing the type of medication. It requires doctors to look closely at when medication effects start to wear off, what the child is doing at those times, what strategies are being used by parents and teachers at those times to encourage effort, and what the child has been eating during the day. On the basis of parent and teacher information, adjustments can include using a "reinforcement" program (e.g., rewards, loss of privileges, etc.) at home and school, providing academic support at school, decreasing the time between doses, increasing dose, and adding additional doses. Let's play out a couple of scenarios. Keep in mind that in each of these illustrations, the child has been thoroughly evaluated by his or her physician for other medical problems that could cause symptoms of inattention, hyperactivity, and impulsivity.

The first scenario reflects a pattern I have seen frequently. It is one in which a child starts taking a medication like Metadate-CD (20 mg). The teacher reports that an 8-year-old boy is improving but is still having difficulties remaining seated, staying quiet, and on task during the day. After school, there is no improvement. In fact, the parents aren't really sure that the medication is helping at all. Review of weekly rating scales indicates that the child's ADHD symptoms are generally viewed as less severe at school, but not at home. The results of the computerized test of attention (e.g., the TOVA) administered two hours after taking Metadate-CD indicate that the child's performance on this test has improved since starting medication and is now consistent with his age group. What would I recommend?

First, I'd want to make sure that the child's dietary patterns include consumption of protein-based foods throughout the day (approximately 15–20 g at each meal, based on USDA recommendations). Why? Because the child is showing deterioration of functioning during the school day and little improvement at home. Consequently, I'd want to ensure that the child is consuming the kinds of foods that can be used to make dopamine and serotonin (a neurotransmitter involved in mood regulation and sleep). Next, I'd ask the teacher to complete a Medication Response Chart for three to five days to find out when the child is beginning to show deterioration of medication effects. Typically, this chart tells me the times of the day when a child is having difficulties.

After identifying the times of day that are most problematic, it is useful to find out what types of activities are occurring at those times. Sometimes, the difficulties are occurring during an activity that is difficult for the child (e.g., doing mathematics problems; completing writing assignments). If these problems are occurring at a time when it is highly unlikely that medication effects have worn off (e.g., within two to three hours after taking Metadate-CD), I'd ask the teacher to see what happens if the child is given a bit more support (e.g., time with a shared aide; pairing with a successful peer role model) or the opportunity to work with computerized word processing or mathematics programs. If the problem is occurring four or more hours after taking Metadate-CD and is occurring during an activity in which the child has shown age appropriate ability, then consideration of a higher dose would appear potentially beneficial.

The choice of medication after school for a child will depend on how long the stimulant seems to be effective and the types of problems displayed. If the child shows positive response during the school day but loses attention or concentration after school (while completing school work), then an increase in dose of sustained release stimulant or administration of a low dose of an immediate release stimulant (e.g., Ritalin or Focalin) after school may prove helpful. However, such an intervention is likely to cause difficulties falling asleep. In those situations, use of anti-hypertensives (e.g., Catapres or Tenex) has been shown to be helpful.

Let's consider another situation. A child begins by taking a low dose of Concerta (18 mg), Metadate-CD (20 mg), or Adderall-XR (5 mg) and no positive response is reported by his teacher or his parents on weekly rating forms. The results of a test of attention (TOVA) continue to indicate that the child is performing significantly poorer than other kids his age. Examination of daily medication response forms shows a high level of inattention, hyperactivity, and impulsivity throughout the day. What to do?

I'd still want to make sure that the child is eating a diet that contains a sufficient amount of protein. If that is the case, then I'd support a clinical trial of a higher dose of stimulant. As is my practice, I would ask parents and teachers to complete weekly behavioral ratings. I also would re-administer the TOVA. If the teacher rating indicated significant improvement and TOVA results revealed a level of performance that was equal to age peers without ADHD, then I would examine the hourly medication response charts. If these charts provided evidence of declining performance during the day (regardless of task), then I would encourage adjustment of medication. If the medication response charts indicated difficulties during completion of a particular task, (e.g., mathematics or writing), I would request evaluation for a specific learning disability, if this type of assessment has not yet been conducted. If the child's performance on the TOVA was still poor, further increase in dose would merit consideration. I'd continue to monitor and evaluate the patient's clinical response, supporting increase in dose until behavior at school was no longer problematic and performance on the TOVA was unimpaired.

WHAT HAPPENS IF MY CHILD DOES NOT
RESPOND OR CAN'T TOLERATE STIMULANTS?

A fairly large percentage of children with ADHD (approximately 15%–30%) either do not respond to methylphenidate (the active ingredient in Ritalin, Concerta, and Metadate-CD) or cannot tolerate this type of medication because of side effects. When the issue is one of insufficient response, it is common to try other types of stimulants (e.g., Adderall-XR or Dexedrine). When the issue is that of inability to tolerate the medication (e.g., because of dramatic loss of appetite, severe sleep disturbance, or development of muscle blinks or twitches called "tics"), other medications may prove helpful. These include norepinephrine specific reuptake inhibitors (e.g., Strattera); "stimulatory" antidepressants (e.g., Imipramine, Effexor, and Wellbutrin); antihypertensives (e.g., Catapres and Tenex); and anticonvulsant medications (e.g., Depakote, Tegretol, and Neurontin). In addition, among my patients who are diagnosed with ADHD but do not show cortical slowing during QEEG evaluation, I also have seen positive response to SSRI-type antidepressants like Zoloft and Lexapro, either alone or in combination with low doses of stimulants like Adderall-XR, Metadate-CD, or Concerta.

Norepinephrine-specific reuptake inhibitors are medications that attempt to increase brain activity by inhibiting the reabsorption of the neurotransmitter, norepinephrine. Because neural pathways that use norepinephrine also activate those brain regions involved in attention, concentration, behavioral control, and social judgment, medications (like Strattera) that enhance the functioning of norepinephrine pathways can also improve the core symptoms of ADHD. This type of medication was developed primarily because of the number of patients who do not respond to stimulant therapy, because of the risk for neuromuscular tics with stimulants, and because of parental concerns about the potential abuse of stimulants.

Stimulatory antidepressant medications like Imipramine, Effexor, and Wellbutrin can be useful in treating patients whose primary ADHD symptoms are inattentive in nature. These medications facilitate the activity of several neurological pathways (including dopaminergic ones) that are involved in attention and mood control. They can enhance attention and also can help by reducing some of the irritability commonly shown by children with ADHD. However, these medications need to be administered for a month or so before you begin to see improvement in your child. Because parents (and their children) hope for more immediate benefits, these medications are typically prescribed when a child is unable to tolerate stimulants or if other medical problems (e.g., bedwetting) are a significant concern. Medications like imipramine can be used in treating enuresis and ADHD and are often helpful in my younger patients.

Antihypertensive medications (Catapres and Tenex) are essentially "blood pressure" medications that can help ADHD patients by reducing symptoms of hyper-activity and impulsivity. They work by occupying brain receptors that are sensitive to the hormone adrenaline. Patients with high blood pressure take these medications to reduce the risk of heart attack that comes with stress. During stressful moments, adrenaline is released by the adrenal glands, causing a variety of physical changes, including increased heart rate and blood pressure. Medications like Catapres and Tenex block the effect of adrenaline, keeping heart rate and blood pressure stable. When taken in low doses by patients with ADHD, these medications seem to reduce hyperactivity. In addition, Catapres appears to reduce the frequency of aggressive outbursts; Tenex seems to reduce obsessive–compulsive symptoms that can occur in ADHD patients. Unfortunately, neither of these medications seems to improve attention.

Anticonvulsant medications (e.g., Tegretol, Depakote, and Neurontin) were initially developed to control seizures. Clinical research has indicated that these medications can treat symptoms of hyperactivity and aggression in children with ADHD who do not respond to stimulant medications. However, because these medications do not improve attention and can adversely affect liver function, they are rarely a "first line" treatment for patients with ADHD.

SSRI-type antidepressants (Zoloft; Paxil) also can be used in the treatment of ADHD patients who do not respond or are unable to tolerate stimulants. Patients diagnosed with ADHD but who do not show cortical slowing on QEEG examination have shown improve-ment in attention, mood, and behavioral control fol-lowing treatment with this type of medication. These medicines work by enhancing the activity of nerve cells that use the neurotransmitter serotonin. Descriptively, neural pathways that use serotonin appear to exert a primary effect on mood. In research efforts, I have seen that Zoloft appears particularly useful for patients with ADHD who tend to lose their temper frequently; Paxil seems to help ADHD patients who are more anxious. I also have seen that a low dose of stimulant medication can be added to these medications to help control hyperactive behaviors. However, caution is advised in the use of SSRIs because recent studies indicate that increased depression can occur when children are treated with SSRI's like Paxil and that withdrawal effects (nausea or flu-like symptoms) can be problem-atic when these medications are discontinued.

Medications for Temper, Anxiety, and Depression

Children with ADHD commonly have problems that go beyond inattention, hyperactivity, and impulsivity. Many of these patients struggle to control their temper, their worries, and their "despair." Parents of children and teens with ADHD can be stunned by the intensity of their child's reactions to disappointment and frustra-tion, alarmed by their child's extensive worries over "nothing," and the degree of despair sometimes shown by these children. Kids with ADHD can become highly explosive when they don't get their way or when they are "punished." They can spend endless hours worrying about disease and disaster. They can talk about "wishing they were dead" or how they are going to "jump out the window" just because you won't take them to Burger King.

Why Does This Happen?

Big question. Little answer. The frontal lobe, as well as other regions of the brain (e.g., the cerebellum, which appears important for social judgment), appears essential in helping people control their emotional reactions. There is a tendency to think that problems in "waking up" the part of the brain that is essential for attention and concentration are limited to forgetting homework and avoiding chores. However, the regions of the brain that are involved in paying attention in school and concentrating on your history homework also are involved in figuring out what to do when mom and dad say "no" or when your brother won't get off the computer. The difficulties a child with ADHD has in "waking" up the frontal lobes will not only contribute to problems learning at school but also contribute to difficulties solving problems at home.

As a result, the medications that were described for treating ADHD also can have a beneficial effect on "mood" problems. Sometimes stimulants help with these problems alone. Sometimes they need to be combined with other medications, such as antidepressants (e.g., Zoloft or Lexapro), antihypertensives (e.g., Catapres or Tenex), or anticonvulsants (e.g., Depakote, Tegretol, or Neurontin). Regardless of the type of medication used, it is important to realize that these medications will help to "tone down" the emotional reaction. However, it will be up to you as well as your child's teachers, counselors, and doctors to teach your child how to learn to effectively express their emotional reactions and solve problems in social situations. Much of this book will concentrate on that process.

What if I Am Not Comfortable With Using Any Type of Medication?

During the past three decades, there has been considerable interest in developing treatments for ADHD that do not require medication. The most promising of these treatments is called EEG biofeedback or neurotherapy. Other treatments that have been studied include social skills training, individual psychotherapy, and family therapy. Although each of these treatments appears to provide some benefit in promoting the social development of children with ADHD, only EEG biofeedback has been associated with improvement in the core symptoms of ADHD. Because of the improvements in attention, impulse control, and academic performance that have been reported in the scientific literature, there has been considerable interest in the use of this type of treatment for ADHD.

Many of the parents who are interested in EEG biofeedback for their children have heard horror stories about medication, worry about the long-term effects of stimulants, have fears that stimulants will turn their children into "junkies," or have seen that these medications do not seem to help. Perhaps they have mistakenly heard that EEG biofeedback cures ADHD. Perhaps they are just hoping that it helps a bit.

Regardless of the reasons why parents are interested in EEG biofeedback, the scientific evidence reported to date indicates that children, teens, and adults with ADHD who are treated with this method improve in a variety of ways. Patients have shown significant gains on computerized tests of attention. Questionnaires completed by parents and teachers indicate significant improvement in the core symptoms of ADHD. Improved scores on tests of intelligence and scholastic abilities also are reported when using this type of treatment. In addition, there is evidence that this treatment results in an improvement in the level of cortical arousal (as measured by QEEG) and that such improvements continue even when medications are discontinued.

How Does EEG Biofeedback Work?

The basic idea behind this therapy is that if a patient is able to learn how to control the level of brain activity in those regions that control attention and planned motor activity, then improvement of attention and reduction of hyperactivity should occur. Patients learn to improve by receiving information (called feedback) in the form of sounds and pictures that are shown on a computer monitor. Essentially, the patient receives a tone and watches video screens change every time he or she produces improved brain activity for one-half of a second. The patient's task is to learn how to produce more of these "half-second" alert periods. As patients do so, improvements in the core symptoms of ADHD have been shown to occur.

While clinical researchers continue to try to understand exactly how this process is learned and how long the improvements will remain, there seems little doubt that clinical gains can and do occur in patients who use this type of therapy. However, because three of the four controlled, group studies published to date permitted parents (and patients) to choose the type of treatment (e.g., medication alone, biofeedback alone, medication combined with biofeedback), it is difficult to determine the percentage of patients who will respond to this type of treatment. Studies examining this question are in process. To find out more about this approach, you can contact the Association for Applied Psychophysiology and Biofeedback (phone: 303-422-8436) or the Society for Neuronal Regulation (phone: 800-488-3867).

Homework

Before you start reading any more of this book, take a few moments to consider the adequacy of your child's medical treatment for ADHD. If she or he is not taking medication, consider some of the options and speak with your child's doctor. If your child is taking medication, complete the two rating forms at the end of this lesson and see how your child's treatment is shaping up. If your child is continuing to have significant problems succeeding at home or school, adjustments are needed. Talk about your concerns with your child's doctor, psychologist, counselor, and teacher. See if you can begin to figure out what is going wrong.

In this lesson, I have tried to provide certain guidelines for you to consider. Use them as best you can but please do not minimize the importance of effective medical intervention. In my treatment of patients with ADHD, I have learned that when properly administered and monitored, medication can be an essential component in the effective treatment of ADHD. Without it, even the most judicious use of reminders and consequences is unlikely to be successful.

My bottom-line advice to you is this: Do not accept that your child is untreatable, and do not tolerate the passage of month after month without improvement. People consult with specialists when "first line" types of treatment fail. Do not hesitate to do so if the standard type of medical care provided by your child's pediatrician or family practitioner is not working. You are not insulting your doctor by asking for a referral to a consultant for a second opinion. Your child's doctor also wants your child to be well.

Just make sure that the "consultant" is a health care provider who specializes in the treatment of ADHD.

Simply because a person is licensed as a psychologist, psychiatrist, or social worker does not mean that he or she is able to provide the range of care needed to treat ADHD. Although you may have some difficulty identifying an "ADHD specialist" in your region, organizations like Children and Adults With Attention-Deficit Hyperactivity Disorder (CH.A.D.D.; phone: 301-306-7070); the clinical psychology, social work, or nursing department at a nearby university; or the social work, psychology, or psychiatry department in a regional teaching hospital, can provide you with some potentially useful leads. If these specialists are located too far from your home to directly treat your child, they may serve as essential members of your child's treatment team, helping to guide pharmacological, psychological, and educational interventions. As you will learn in this book, effective treatment of ADHD requires medical interventions, adequate nutrition, school-based accommodation and remediation, systematic use of effective parenting strategies, and training in the development of attention and other social skills.

MEDICATION TOLERANCE CHECKLIST

CHILD'S NAME: _____

BIRTH DATE: _____

MEDICATION: _____ DOSE: _____

TIMES GIVEN: ___ AM ___ AM ___ PM ___ PM

WHICH OF THESE SYMPTOMS ARE BEING SHOWN BY YOUR CHILD?

1. _____ runs about uncontrollably at home in the morning
2. _____ runs about uncontrollably at home in the afternoon
3. _____ runs about uncontrollably at home in the evening
4. _____ appears to be "in a fog" or "dazed" in the morning
5. _____ appears to be "in a fog" or "dazed" in the afternoon
6. _____ appears to be "in a fog" or "dazed" in the evening
7. _____ seems more likely to cry than usual
8. _____ seems more likely to throw objects, yell at, or hit people than usual
9. _____ has little or no appetite
10. _____ is having more difficulty falling asleep at night
11. _____ has stomach pain or discomfort
12. _____ has headaches
13. _____ is drowsy during the day
14. _____ complains of a "dry mouth"
15. _____ is "wetting" the bed at night

Other concerns: _____
_____
_____
_____
_____
_____

MEDICATION RESPONSE CHART

PATIENT'S NAME: **DATE:**

RATER: _____

PLEASE CHECK <u>ONLY</u> WHEN A PROBLEM OCCURS

Behavior	Time of Day								
	8AM	9AM	10AM	11AM	12N	1PM	2PM	3–5PM	6–8PM

Did not listen:
  A little
  A lot									

Interrupts:
  A little
  A lot									

Off task:
  A little
  A lot									

Out of seat:
  A little
  A lot									

Noisy:
  A little
  A lot									

Moody:
  A little
  A lot									

Hits/Pushes
  A little
  A lot									

Argues:
  A little
  A lot									

Please complete both of these forms daily for 5 days.

Fax to _____ at the following number:

4

Nutrition Does Matter

In this lesson, I want to focus on the dietary habits of your child and how they relate to attention, impulsivity, and hyperactivity. Why? Is it because I think that ADHD is caused by inadequate nutrition? No, that's not the reason, although there is evidence that children who have deficiencies of iron, zinc, and magnesium will show symptoms of inattention, impulsivity, and hyperactivity. Is it because I think that food allergies cause ADHD? Again, the answer is no, although there are well-controlled studies that indicate that symptoms that mimic ADHD can be caused by allergic reactions to foods like wheat, corn, soy, eggs, milk, and certain food dyes and additives.

There are several reasons why it is important for you to understand how foods contribute to a person's ability to attend, inhibit impulsive behaviors, analyze information, regulate emotional responses, and solve problems. Our selection of foods will determine whether we have the capacity to manufacture the essential neurotransmitters necessary for brain functions. What we eat will determine whether we will have the materials necessary to manufacture the enzymes, cells, and tissues essential for life functions. In addition, should we mistakenly eat foods that cause allergic reactions, our ability to attend, think, and control our emotions will be compromised. Because of this, I routinely request that all of my patients be screened for common food allergies prior to initiating medication for ADHD or making specific dietary recommendations to address nutritional deficiencies.

WHAT KINDS OF NUTRIENTS ARE IMPORTANT FOR THE BRAIN?

This is a very important and complex question. I'll try to limit what I review to those types of nutrients that have been investigated in controlled, clinical studies of patients who present with symptoms of inattention and hyperactivity. The most critical appear to be the amino acids tyrosine, tryptophan, and phenylalanine (derived from protein-based foods), minerals (like iron, zinc, and magnesium), and essential fatty acids (EFAs). That is not to say that we do not need to consume foods that contain calcium, sodium, and potassium and other nutrients. It is just important that you realize that deficiencies of certain types of foods can contribute to some of the problems commonly shown by patients with ADHD.

Let's start with proteins. The most common sources of protein are beef, pork, poultry, fish, eggs, beans, nuts, and dairy products. These foods are absorbed by our bodies and used to make neurotransmitters, the chemicals released by our brain cells to communicate with each other so that we can pay attention, learn, solve problems, control our emotional reactions, and do all the other tasks essential for our survival. Without a sufficient amount of protein, it is impossible to pay attention, control our actions, and regulate our moods. Because our bodies immediately begin to make "brain awakening" neurotransmitters when you eat protein, a good idea is to start your day with a breakfast that includes milk, cheese, eggs, meat, peanut butter, and soy-based breakfast drinks or bars.

What about minerals? We have learned that deficiencies of several different minerals can cause symptoms of inattention, impulsivity, and hyperactivity. The minerals that have primarily been studied are iron, zinc, and magnesium. Let's start with iron because it is a mineral that may be more familiar to you.

Iron is a mineral that can be obtained from eating a variety of foods. Although spinach has been famous as a good source of iron since the days of the classic cartoon, "Popeye," it is far from the only food that can help us take in our daily requirements of this mineral. Certain cereals (e.g., Cheerios, Frosted Mini-Wheats, Total), meats (beef, turkey), vegetables (e.g., peas), and starches (e.g., potatoes) contain iron. Why worry about iron intake? Iron is important for our brains because it directly relates to oxygen flow to the brain. Without oxygen, brain cells are unable to function and will die. Iron is also involved in the production of certain enzymes that are needed to make neurotransmitters like dopamine and serotonin.

Zinc is a mineral that has become a more familiar topic over the past few years, particularly for its role in fighting colds, flus, and infection. Like iron, zinc can be found in such cereals as Cheerios, Wheaties, Total, Product 19, and even sugary ones like Cap'n Crunch's Peanut Butter Crunch and Cinnamon Toast Crunch. It also can be found in foods like beef, beans, turkey, chicken, pork, lamb, oysters, and crabs. Zinc is an essential ingredient in the development of numerous enzymes, including those that make our neurotransmitters.

Magnesium is a mineral that (like zinc) is involved in hundreds of enzyme activities. In fact, it has been identified in more than 300 enzyme activities (about half of the known metabolic processes in our bodies). Among the substances that are developed from magnesium are the myelin sheath that surrounds our brain cells (making it possible for neural transmission) and the neurotransmitters involved in attention and concentration. Like other minerals, magnesium is found in meats, nuts, soybeans, and the ever popular spinach.

Essential fatty acids (EFAs) also are important for maintaining attention. They include linoleic acid and alpha-linoleic acids and must be eaten because the body cannot synthesize them. The "n-3" (Omega-3) fatty acids are used to build and repair the myelin sheath that surrounds nerve cells. Fish and nuts are an excellent source of EFAs.

What Are My Kids Supposed to Eat?

In some ways, you are already an expert on the issue of food and attention. Think about it. What happens if you get up and don't have time to eat breakfast and still get to work by eight o'clock? What will you do? Eat a carrot? Nope, not likely. Reach for a cigarette and a cup of coffee? Maybe. Grab a donut? A soda? Again, fairly likely. Why? Because they help you feel more alert . . . for a little while.

When you are feeling sluggish, nothing cures the sense of fatigue and lack of mental energy like some carbohydrates (cereal, bagel, muffin), sugary foods (donut, cookie, candy bar), some caffeine, or some nicotine. Maybe you didn't realize that sugars can be absorbed by brain cells, causing them to become more active. Maybe you didn't know that caffeine and nicotine are central nervous system stimulants that cause an increase in alertness. You might not have known, but your body did. Your body also knew that eating a carrot does not immediately increase the activity of brain cells. So there aren't too many of us munching on those in the morning.

However, what most people don't realize is that when they bite into that first donut or munch on a spoonful of cereal, or sip that sugar-laden cup of coffee, they are setting off a complex series of chemical reactions in the body that will lead them to feel more drowsy within an hour or so. When we first eat or drink carbohydrates (cereals, breads, sugary drinks), sugars head for the brain, providing that immediate pick-me-up. However, the body senses the arrival of these sugars and starts releasing insulin (to break down the sugars so they don't cause damage). The release of insulin causes the brain to begin to manufacture more serotonin (a neurotransmitter that at elevated levels causes sedation and sleepiness). Within an hour or so, you're reaching for another cup of coffee or bun to charge you up again.

Let's shift to lunch. What happens then? Well, for most people, lunch is the first time that they eat any protein. In fact, for many, lunch is the first time that they eat anything other than carbohydrates or sugary sweet drinks (e.g., coffee). So we head to the various burger worlds, pizza places, or other nearby neighborhood quick eateries to munch. Now, I know we want to believe that because we're finally eating all this good stuff (fruits, vegetables, chicken, beef, fish, beans, and breads), after lunch we'll be raring to go. But, as you well know, if we've skipped breakfast, we're in a food coma an hour after lunch.

Hey, our bodies have to take time to process all that stuff, and it naturally asks for blood to head to the digestive track (which means away from your brain), which is one of the reasons why you're so sluggish. So it's back to caffeine, sugars, and nicotine to survive until we gorge at dinner time and beyond.

Which brings us to the endless feasting that occurs for many of us after we get home. Many of us will eat while cooking (or waiting for the cooking to be done), have our largest meal of the day at a time our body is preparing to go to sleep, and then wonder why we can't get to sleep until it's midnight (or later). Although we may realize that it's highly unlikely that a body recently filled with sugars (that includes cereals and juices) and caffeine (coffee, colas, chocolate) will be ready to sleep, these foods taste so good and *we deserve to have some fun*, right?! After we finally get to sleep, we find the alarm going off so early that of course we're not hungry for breakfast. We're mentally and physically fatigued (which certainly doesn't help us concentrate and pay attention). So, we gulp down a glass of juice or cup of coffee and the cycle begins again.

The lesson to be learned from all of this is that starting off the day by not eating any protein sets the stage for impaired attention and concentration. In order for your child to have a chance at being attentive during the morning and throughout the day, nutrition will matter, beginning with breakfast.

So, What Do the Experts Recommend?

Most of us are aware that there are governmental agencies that conduct dietary research and are responsible for advising Americans about healthy food choices. Graphic illustrations like the "Food Pyramid" appear on cereal boxes and food wrappers and inform us of the nutritional contents of pretty much everything we eat. The problem is, few of us know if a breakfast of Cap'n Crunch (.75 cup) and milk (8 oz), a lunch of pizza (2 slices) and a soda (12 oz), an after school snack of Doritos (1 oz) and a soda (12 oz), and spaghetti (1 cup) and meatballs (3.5 oz) with a glass of milk (8 oz) for dinner, would be considered sufficient for a 10-year-old boy weighing 100 pounds. What's your guess? Let's do a simple analysis.

I'll use a standard textbook to determine what is in each of these foods (*Bowes & Church's Food Values of Portions Commonly Used*, Philadelphia: J.B. Lippincott, 1994) and then compare our results with *Recommended Dietary Allowances*, authored by the Food and Nutrition Board of the National Academy of Sciences (Washington, DC: National Academy Press, 1989). If you don't happen to have a personal copy of these books (who does?), you can find this information at www.nal.usda.gov. There, the United States Department of Agriculture (USDA) publishes the *National Nutrient Database for Standard Reference*. Here is the food comparison:

Daily Food Chart: 10-Year-Old Boy

Food Content Analysis	Tryptophan mg	Phenylalanine mg	Tyrosine mg	Iron mg	Zinc mg	Magnesium mg
Breakfast:						
Cap'n Crunch	12	76	59	4.81	2.37	10
Milk	113	388	380	0.12	0.95	34
Lunch:						
Pizza (2 slices)	182	732	696	1.16	1.64	32
Soda	0	0	0	0	0	0
Snack:						
Doritos	14	99	82	0.43	0.43	25
Soda	0	0	0	0	0	0
Dinner:						
Spaghetti	85	324	175	1.96	0.74	25
Meatballs	302	929	764	2.10	5.40	20
Milk	113	388	388	0.12	0.95	34
Total Consumed	**821**	**2936**	**2552**	**10.70**	**12.48**	**180**
Advised	**150**	**500**	**500**	**10.00**	**10.00**	**170**

What does this mean? Well, even though our 10-year-old's diet was pretty heavy in terms of calories and fat, his diet actually exceeds recommended levels for amino acids and minerals. While his dietary plan may be far from ideal, it at least contains certain nutrients necessary for brain functioning. The down-side is that little was eaten at breakfast.

To help you begin to analyze the adequacy of your child's diet, let's consider the government's "recommendations" with respect to four basic nutrients that are involved in promoting attention and behavioral control. These nutrients are protein, iron, magnesium, and zinc. The following chart also is derived from *Recommended Dietary Allowances* by the Food and Nutrition Board.

Recommended Dietary Allowances for Protein, Magnesium, Iron, and Zinc

Group	Age (yrs)	Protein (g)	Mag. (mg)	Iron (mg)	Zinc (mg)
Children	4–6	24	120	10	10
Children	7–10	28	170	10	10
Males	11–14	45	270	12	15
Males	15–18	59	400	12	15
Males	19–24	58	350	10	15
Females	11–14	46	280	15	12
Females	15–18	44	300	15	12
Females	19–24	46	280	15	12

Note. Data from *Recommended Dietary Allowances*, by the Food and Nutrition Board, 1989.

As you review this chart, please realize that it is intended to provide a general guideline. Specific dietary recommendations are linked to an individual's height and weight. A consultation with a registered dietician is probably wise if you want a thorough analysis of the adequacy of your child's diet. However, if I start examining diet with that type of detail in this book, you're probably going to get lost. Let's try to keep it simple.

How Can I Use These Charts?

A good place to begin is to keep a simple food log for 3 days. Just so you don't get overwhelmed, start on a weekend. Write down everything your child eats. Try to be as accurate as possible (e.g., the number of ounces or grams) when you record each food consumed. Next, begin to calculate how much protein, magnesium, iron, and zinc your child ate. Sometimes the information will be provided on the food wrapper. Sometimes it won't. To help you in your work, it would probably be a good idea to go to the library or search the Internet (www.nal.usda.gov) so you can refer to the list of *Recommended Dietary Allowances* and look at the USDA *National Nutrient Database for Standard Reference*. That is basically how I found this information. The simplest way to use the chart is to establish a family rule that your child is to eat approximately one-third of the recommended protein at breakfast and one-third at lunch. That way, his or her body will begin to get the raw material needed to promote sustained attention in the beginning of the day.

Once again, I'd say that if you get overwhelmed trying to do this kind of analysis, give yourself a break and obtain an evaluation from a registered dietician. This type of consultation won't cost you a lot of money and is likely to provide you with useful information, as well as with some strategies for improving your child's diet. If the goal is to improve your child's attention and impulse control, you need to make sure they are eating the kinds of foods that will help them develop these skills. No amount of medication, parenting, school intervention, or counseling will correct an attentional problem that is caused by nutritional deficiency.

What if My Kid Won't Eat Anything Worthwhile?

This is probably the most common complaint I hear from the parents of my patients. I wish I could tell you that if you just ignored the issue, it would go away. It doesn't. In the thousands of kids I have treated, I have rarely met a child who ate a sufficient amount of protein at breakfast and at lunch. A lot of my kids are pretty much zombies in the morning and get so distracted by the activity in the cafeteria that they forget to eat. In addition, the appetite of kids who are being treated with stimulant will be suppressed because of medication effects.

So, to get things moving in the right direction, you will need to make a decision. If you accept the scientific evidence that indicates that the brain actually needs foods that provide essential amino acids, vitamins, and minerals, then you will need to make eating a nutritious breakfast and lunch one of the lessons to be learned in life. While your child will need to be involved in choosing protein rich foods that will provide a variety of amino acids and minerals, you will need to establish the ground rules. In some ways, family rules about nutrition are going to sound similar to those you probably have for bathing, brushing teeth, and bedtime. Just as brushing teeth, taking a shower, and getting enough sleep are essential, so is eating a nutritious breakfast. As with these other areas, choosing not to follow mom's and dad's rules is not "okay." Your child will need to learn that the use of certain electronic devices (television, computer, video games) and permission to engage in desirable activities (playing outside, visiting friends, going to baseball or soccer practice, attending dance class) is linked to dietary habits. I often have said to kids, "If your brain is on 'E' because you haven't fed it enough protein, then you really should be resting."

PROTEIN-RICH FOODS THAT KIDS WITH ADHD MIGHT EAT IN THE MORNING

One truism about kids with ADHD is that nothing works forever. As you know, these kids might love a particular food for 3 days straight and then tire of it. The following list comes from my patients. You might find some foods that appeal to your child:

Meats: Sausage links, sausage biscuits, bacon, "slim jims," and chicken nuggets are "okay" with many of my kids. In a rush, a slice of deli ham, turkey, or chicken can work. Each ounce of meat provides about seven grams of protein.

Eggs: A couple of eggs (cooked any way that will go down) is a good way to get started. You can cut the white portion of a hard-boiled egg into soft, little protein chunks. An egg white provides about seven grams of protein.

Dairy: An eight-ounce glass of milk beats walking out the door with nothing in the stomach (it provides about seven grams of protein). Cheese sticks go down pretty well and every ounce of cheese provides about seven grams. Yogurt is also easily tolerated and you can boost the protein level by mixing in some protein powder or a little dry milk. Cheese sandwiches (grilled or not) may also be a winner. I often gross out my patients with my morning favorite: cold lasagna. Pizza (in all the varieties) can work as well.

Nuts: Peanut butter on toast, muffin, or bagel isn't too tough a sell. Kids can smear on all the jelly or marshmallow fluff they want. Some kids will prefer just munching on nuts. You'd be surprised how few nuts make up a serving (about 15 nuts or 2 tablespoons of peanut butter provide about seven grams of protein).

Soy: There are a number of protein powders available for mixing in drinks and using in recipes. VERY

FEW of my patients can tolerate a drink made from those "body building" type powders (too chalky, the kids feel like they are gagging). The same is true for most protein bars (too dense for most kids), although some of my patients do think the Snicker's Marathon Bar is pretty tasty.

That being said, soy-based powders are among the most useful at home. I often recommend having a container of soy powder in the cupboard. I encourage parents to think of it as just another cooking ingredient. Many of my patients have parents who will combine soy powder with wheat flour, sugar, baking powder, and other ingredients to make high-protein chocolate chip cookies, muffins, brownies, and a variety of fruit breads (apple, banana). This is one of the easiest ways to get 10-20 grams of protein into your child. These "treats" are easily transportable to school for lunch and snack. Just make sure that your soy powder can be used in cooking and that your child isn't allergic to soy.

My favorite recipe combines several of these protein sources and was created by one of my patients. Let's call it Sean's Breakfast Surprise. It is created from the following ingredients: chocolate pudding, soy protein powder, Cool Whip, and crushed Oreo cookies. He washes this down with a glass of milk and it has great staying power. It is also quite high in protein content. I mention it so you begin to get the idea that I'm hoping breakfast can be a bit more creative. I'm not rooting for this to be a battle. I hope that as you review the food ideas for breakfast you and your child will hit on some that will work.

Isn't It a Bad Idea to Make an Issue Out of Eating?

No! Teaching your children about healthy choices is one of a parent's primary roles in life. When parents tell me they are worried that their child will develop an eating disorder because they are insisting on a nutritious breakfast, I usually ask them if they believe their child will become obsessive or compulsive if they make sure the child takes a bath, brushes his or her teeth, or changes into clean clothes. Obviously there are extreme and abusive methods for teaching lessons about nutrition or cleanliness. I'm not advocating that you make meal time an anxiety-provoking experience. I'm simply talking about using common reinforcement strategies to encourage your child to learn an important lesson from their parents: "nutrition does count."

What About Allergies?

A review of the scientific literature reveals that there are well-controlled studies that report certain children are sensitive (and become inattentive or hyperactive) when exposed to certain food dyes and preservatives. Other studies indicate that some children demonstrate symptoms of ADHD after ingesting certain foods (e.g., corn or wheat). If you notice that your child's attention or behavior worsens after eating a specific food, a consultation with an allergist (particularly one familiar with behavioral issues) may be beneficial. The Feingold Association (www.feingold.org) is another excellent source of information on this topic.

HOMEWORK

Take a look at the protein content contained in your child's breakfast. Compare it to the recommended amount. Then have a conversation with your child about the need to have the recommended amount for breakfast each day. Talk with them about the kinds of foods that can provide the necessary protein. Let them help you to decide on the foods that will be available at breakfast. However, let them know that the new family rule is that they need to eat a nutritious breakfast to have the energy (and your permission) to engage in certain activities. While I'll be talking about the whole issue of "motivating" kids with ADHD in later chapters, see how you do in motivating your child to improve his or her diet. Remember, to learn a new skill a child not only needs to be shown (or told) the lesson. They also need a reason to try the new skill. That's where motivation comes in.

5

Students With ADHD
Are Entitled to Help at School

One of the most frustrating experiences parents face is the ongoing problem of trying to help children with ADHD succeed in school. Very few children diagnosed with ADHD are able to succeed in school without some type of support. For some children, the support is provided by a parent who stays on top of the child from the minute the kid hits the door after school until the time she or he goes to sleep. These parents repeatedly remind the child about homework assignments and plead, argue, fight, punish, praise, and exhaust themselves in an effort to make sure that homework is completed.

For other children, support comes from an understanding teacher who recognizes that the student has problems listening to instructions, remembering assignments, concentrating while reading and writing, organizing books and homework, and keeping up with long-term projects. These teachers independently make "accommodations," kindly developing ways for the student with ADHD to be successful without humiliating or criticizing the child. Such educators have recognized that ADHD is a disabling medical condition, just like hearing or visual loss. They have incorporated the knowledge that led our government to determine that ADHD was a "health impairment" and treat children who have ADHD with the same kind of respect and compassion that would be given to a child who has difficulty in school because of a hearing or visual problem. These teachers are a blessing for kids with ADHD because they recognize that repeated school failure does not breed success. They well know that it leads a child to stop trying, and perhaps "drop out" of school.

However, despite two federal laws (Individuals With Disabilities Education Act, or IDEA, and Section 504 of the Rehabilitation Act of 1973), which specify that children with ADHD are entitled to academic support and accommodation, many children with this disorder do not receive any type of support. I'll give you an example of how this typically happens. I'll use a patient of mine I'll call "Mike" as an example. His story is similar to the stories of thousands of teens with ADHD that I have heard.

As you read "Mike's Tale," you might consider it to be a bit extreme. However, his story is far more representative of what occurs in clinical practice than you would think. It is the story of a "hyperactive" and "impulsive child" who was never diagnosed with ADHD. A similar tale could be told of the "inattentive" child (often a girl) who "daydreamed" her way through the primary and secondary grades, never realizing her intelligence and never experiencing the satisfaction that comes with school success because she, too, was never diagnosed with ADHD.

Mike came with his parents to my clinic during the tenth grade. He was failing math, science, social studies, Spanish, and English. He did not complete assignments, did not study for tests and routinely cut classes. Because of his illegal absences from class, he would routinely be placed in "in-school suspension," reporting to a specific room in the school where he was to remain all day. However, he would feel restless being cooped up in such a place and would avoid going there. As a result, further disciplinary action would occur, typically "out-of-school suspension," which is like getting a week of school vacation as a reward for misbehavior.

Of course, Mike's school problems were not limited to merely cutting classes and getting bad grades. He made jokes and talked in class, interrupting the teacher and other students. He also showed little interest in class activities. But none of this is what brought Mike to my clinic. What did? His temper.

In many schools across the country, the junior and senior high school years are times when a kid has to handle a lot of hassles. Most of us don't have to deal with someone teasing or threatening us at work on a day-to-day basis. Our country has laws against those kinds of behaviors. However, kids in grades 7 to 12 (and to be honest, in the earlier grades as well) often face daily mocking comments, social isolation, and verbal and physical threats. If you're a kid with ADHD (meaning a child with impulse control problems and impaired ability to concentrate in order to solve problems), you are going to have a hard time with this kind of treatment, and it is very likely that you will be subjected to some type of disciplinary action because of impaired impulse control. That's what happened to Mike.

In Mike's case, someone made one too many wisecracks in a classroom. Mike threw some tables and chairs and was headed for the kid, threatening to kill him. Not a smart thing to do. The net result: Mike was expelled from school, pending consultation with a doctor like me. His parents and teachers were unsure what was wrong. Some thought he was emotionally disturbed and needed to be placed in a hospital for intensive treatment. Some thought he was "on drugs." Others felt he was depressed. The ever popular "Oppositional Defiant Disorder" was also suggested as an explanation for his academic and social problems. Perhaps it was his parents' fault for being too easy on Mike. Not a single teacher suggested ADHD. If they had taken a look at his academic history, all of them would have.

Mike's kindergarten teacher initially noted that he was a kid who had difficulty remaining seated, particularly during group activities. He would interrupt instruction, provide answers before questions were completed, and intrude on others as they worked. He seemed to have a hard time listening and needed to be busy. She recognized his intelligence and considered him to be an "enthusiastic" student who needed to slow down a bit.

During the primary grades, Mike continued to display difficulties remaining on task during group instruction. He was fidgety in his seat and had to be reminded to be quiet during instruction. His desk was a mess and he had a hard time finding materials. He forgot papers that needed to get to his parents and lost homework that needed to be returned to his teachers. However, the results of standardized tests of academic skills indicated that he was a bright child, with no evidence of a learning disorder. His teachers thought so too, although his work was sloppy and his handwriting was hard to decipher. During these years, he was considered to be an intelligent child who needed to concentrate and work harder. His parents were given the impression that Mike "could do better if he tried." Mike began to be punished at home for failing to "do his best" but the punishment did little to change his behavior or performance at school.

By the time Mike hit the third and fourth grades, teachers were no longer making positive comments on his report cards. Rather, he would learn that his report card marks were lowered by his failure to complete assignments. He was told that he needed to work harder. His report cards would include long checklists of "skills needing improvement" (e.g., does not listen, does not complete work assigned in class, lacks self-control). His work continued to be "sloppy," and his lack of motivation was cause for concern.

During this time, daily notes were exchanged between parents and teachers about assignments, and each day was a battle between Mike and his parents. To get Mike to complete his work, one of his parents would literally have to sit with him. The parent would need to prompt Mike repeatedly to do his work. However, Mike would complain that he didn't know what to do or how to find the answers to the questions in English, science, or social studies. Getting some kind of answer on paper was even more of a problem. Mike would drive his parents crazy by his inability to recognize an answer, even when they pointed out the information in his book. His one-to-three-word answers came after hours of work. Even more frustrating . . . after all the time and effort expended by his parents, Mike often lost his homework. In addition, his lack of knowledge of basic facts made completing his math homework a task in creative guessing.

During junior high, the bottom fell out. He had a different teacher for each subject. His lack of interest in schoolwork, his failure to complete assignments, and his low test scores resulted in failing grades. His classroom interruptions were no longer considered evidence of intelligence and enthusiasm. They simply resulted in disciplinary actions. Progress notes from teachers indicated that he needed to pay attention, study harder, and complete his work. Junior high is the time when kids need to take responsibility for their actions! If Mike did not make the effort, then he would fail and attend summer school. Maybe failure and spending part of his summer vacation in school would turn the tide. Of course, it didn't.

When you review these teacher comments, nearly every one of Mike's teachers from kindergarten on up noticed that this child had difficulty attending to instruction, concentrating on school tasks, completing work, organizing his materials, and controlling impulsive behavior. Yet he was never identified as a student with ADHD. One question screams for an answer:

How Did Mike's ADHD Go Undiagnosed for so Long?

Although there are many ways this question could be answered, I think it boils down to the lack of what doctors call a "diagnostic formulation." Let me tell you what a "diagnostic formulation" is. It's a fancy way to answer the question, "Why is this person having these problems?" In Mike's case, no qualified health care professional was asked to conduct a thorough evaluation to determine the causes of his ADHD symptoms until he was 16 years old. Without such an evaluation and "diagnostic formulation," children with any kind of medical problem will continue to struggle with their symptoms. That shouldn't surprise anyone, whether we are talking about visual or hearing impairments, respiratory or heart problems, or attentional and impulse control disorders.

When we are talking about children who show symptoms of inattention, hyperactivity, and impulsivity, parents and teachers try to determine why the child is not succeeding. That is understandable. It certainly makes sense that for a 6-month period, teachers and parents explore issues like academic skill development, maturity, and motivation as they attempt to improve a child's attention, concentration, and behavioral control. However, if ADHD symptoms have persisted in a child 4 years old or older for longer than 6 months, despite the best effort of parents and teachers, and it is the opinion of the teacher that the child's inattention or lack of behavioral control is interfering with learning, it is time to seek an evaluation by a qualified health care specialist.

The reasons for evaluation by a psychologist, clinical social worker, or physician (usually a pediatrician or a psychiatrist) go back to the idea of a diagnostic formulation. Teachers can evaluate a child's abilities in reading, mathematics, and written expression, helping to identify children who are not "paying attention" because of learning disabilities. They also can provide valuable information regarding a child's behavior and functioning in the class. By doing so, they can assist a doctor in determining the presence of ADHD symptoms in the classroom. However, as I reviewed in previous lessons, symptoms of inattention or hyperactivity can be caused by a variety of medical conditions, including ADHD. Teachers are not certified to diagnose the reasons a child is displaying symptoms of inattention, impulsivity, or hyperactivity; doctors are. It simply is not appropriate for teachers to be placed (or to place themselves) in a position to diagnose ADHD. They do not have the training, the expertise, or the professional license to do so.

How Can I Get My Kid Help in School?

After your child is diagnosed with ADHD by a qualified health care professional, he or she can receive assistance at school for problems with attention and behavioral control. It is important for you to realize that the federal government considers ADHD to be a health condition that can impair "alertness" (IDEA, 1998 Revision) as well as a medical–psychiatric condition that impairs the significant life function that is learning (Section 504 of the Rehabilitation Act of 1973). Because of the preponderance of scientific evidence that ADHD is "real," federal laws require school districts to systematically evaluate children *who have been diagnosed with ADHD* to determine the ways their health problems are interfering with learning. Before I get into specific ways to help your child, I'd like to briefly summarize these laws so you better understand the "educational rights" of children with ADHD.

Individuals With Disabilities Education Act, 1998 Revision

This federal law was developed so children with disabilities can participate in an educational program that will promote their success. The law provides funds for school districts to provide specialized educational services for children who have learning disabilities, serious emotional problems, mental retardation, traumatic brain injury, vision or hearing impairments, physical disabilities, or "other health problems" like ADHD. For a child with ADHD to qualify for supportive services under IDEA, two important conditions must be met. First, the child must be diagnosed with ADHD by a person qualified to do so (e.g., licensed psychologist, social worker, or physician). Second, the ADHD symptoms must be shown to limit alertness to academic tasks and adversely affect educational performance. This is where all those teacher comments on report cards, assignment workbooks, and "failure notices" can be used to help qualify your child for assistance.

The revision of the IDEA that defined ADHD as a "health impairment" represented a significant step forward in efforts to help students with ADHD. Prior to the 1998 revision, some school districts insisted that the child had to be diagnosed with a specific learning disability to receive services. As a result, when parents requested an evaluation for their child with ADHD, tests of intelligence and academic skills were performed. If the results of the testing did not reveal a disability of reading, mathematical, or writing skills, no services were provided. Rarely did school districts inform parents that their children qualified for "accommodation" under another federal law (The Rehabilitation Act of 1973, Section 504). As a result, neither remediation nor accommodation was provided to these children.

The revised IDEA clearly states that ADHD is a health impairment and that children do not need to show evidence of a learning disability on standardized tests to qualify for services. Rather, just as with children who are deaf or blind, children with ADHD are entitled to a "functional assessment." School districts are required to thoroughly assess how a child's attentional problems or impulsivity–hyperactivity are interfering with educational performance and to develop an educational plan of instruction and accommodation that is sufficient for the child to succeed in school. Let's take a minute to think through this by comparing a patient with ADHD and one who is not succeeding because of a hearing loss.

Picture yourself as the parent of a child whose hearing is significantly impaired. You know that your child has difficulty listening and cannot follow verbal instructions, but sometimes he seems as though he understands what you're talking about. Let's pretend that this child somehow ends up in school and no one knows that she or he had a hearing loss. The child might move about the class, unaware that the teacher is asking him or her to sit down. The child would not hear the teacher's instructions and would not "remember." This forgetfulness would lead to reprimands (and disciplinary action) from the teacher, failure to complete assignments, and poor marks on the report card.

If you and the teacher followed my "6-month" rule, your child would be evaluated by a physician or other specialist and the hearing loss would be identified. This information would be shared with your child's school district and an Individual Education Plan (IEP) would be developed.

After the plan was developed and implemented in the classroom, life would greatly change for the better. No longer would you and the teacher discuss whether the child's "inattention," poor academic performance, or "wandering" in class was because of a lack of motivation, immaturity, or "poor parenting." Instead, you and the teacher would accept the "diagnostic formulation" of a hearing loss. Your child would no longer be required to "listen" in order to get instruction. The child would not be told that "third graders should be able to remember what their teachers say" and to "try harder." Assistive technology (e.g., amplification of the teacher's voice; use of hearing aids) might be used. Instruction given verbally also could be provided in a written form. Testing modifications (e.g., use of written tests only) also might be provided. In short, any and all reasonable accommodations and interventions would be provided so your child's hearing loss would not interfere with learning essential academic skills.

Now let's imagine your child has problems in attending that are not due to a hearing loss. Let's say you consulted with a doctor and learned that the child's inattention was caused by a different health impairment, ADHD. Now what? Well, just as with a hearing loss, the school district would need to be informed of the diagnosis. And, just as with a hearing loss, the school district would need to conduct a thorough evaluation of the ways ADHD was affecting the child's functioning and provide assistance.

This means that parents of children with ADHD no longer need to accept that a school will not provide assistance because the "test results" showed that their children did not have a learning disability. All too often, parents have accepted that their child simply needs to "try harder to control themselves" and "try to pay attention." From my perspective (and that of the federal government), that would be the same as telling a hearing-impaired child that he or she needed to try to listen better, or a visually impaired child that she or he needs to try to see better. Kids with hearing or visual impairments are entitled to better treatment! So are kids with ADHD!

What Kind of Help is Available for Children With ADHD?

A lot. I'll give you a brief overview now and get specific later in the lesson. Children with ADHD are likely to have specific disabilities in reading, mathematics, and written expression. For those children, part of their educational program will involve efforts to improve those skills. They may participate in remedial reading, writing, or mathematics programs or be tutored in those skills. However, until their skills in these core areas are equal to grade expectations, specialized instruction and accommodation need to be provided.

For example, children with ADHD who also display significant problems on tests of reading skills won't succeed if they are given one period of remedial reading per day and are then sent home to read their seventh grade social studies book, search for the answers to the questions listed in the back of their chapter, and write down the answers for the 20 homework questions. If their reading ability is impaired, then their educational program must include not only remediation, but also accommodation (or adjustments). The same holds true if the disability is in the area of mathematics or written expression. A listing of many of these accommodations is provided at the end of this lesson.

Whereas many children with ADHD have specific learning disabilities, some do not. These children have academic problems that are not directly related to their ability to read, write, or answer math problems per se. Rather, these children have difficulties attending to instruction, concentrating while reading, and thinking while writing. In addition, children with ADHD are easily distracted by other children and activities in and around the classroom. They "drift off" and do not hear the teacher's instructions. They find it is difficult to remain in their seats. They interrupt the teacher and other children. They are unable to concentrate or complete seat work like other children, and they end up losing recess time or have to stay after school to complete this work. They find that they cannot write as quickly and neatly as others and end up having to "redo" their work. They struggle to succeed in so many ways . . . and there are so many ways that you and their school can help.

Both remediation and accommodation are the keys to succeeding in school. A teacher has every right to decide that she or he will try to help students learn essential facts in social studies by asking them to find the answers to a list of questions. However, if a child has ADHD, this instructional method will need to be modified to accommodate the child's disabilities. Just as a teacher would not be likely to ask a hearing impaired student to take notes in class and study them for a test, a teacher of a student with ADHD is required to make similar accommodations.

When I speak with parents and teachers about such accommodations, there is often a sense of resistance. Sometimes, the hesitancy is framed as "we can't continue to baby this student." Sometimes, it is expressed as "students in the fifth grade are required to . . ." Sometimes, it is stated as "the student has to learn how to do this sooner or later . . . they won't give him this type of help in college." Each of these statements reflects a lack of recognition of ADHD as a health impairment.

Would you say to a deaf child, "Look, sooner or later you're going to have to hear. So we are not going to give you class notes in written form."? Would you say to a visually impaired child, "Look, you have got to work harder at reading. You're not going to be able to get books on tape forever."? Of course not.

When this same type of reasoning is applied to kids with ADHD, there seems to be an emotional reaction. Sort of like, "Yes, I recognize that the student has ADHD, but he needs to learn how to take his own notes in class." My response is that it would be great if the student can learn how to take notes in class. The student should be taught how to do that. However, until the student demonstrates sufficient ability in that area, the child is entitled to receive assistance. *To say that a 15-year-old student with ADHD "should be able to take notes, organize materials, prepare study guides, study for exams, comprehend literature, and write coherent essays" is the equivalent of saying that a visually impaired student should be able to see by the age of 15 years.*

ADHD is a health impairment that has been shown to endure into adulthood. While individuals with ADHD can learn essential academic skills, they do not develop them at the same rate as their peers, nor do they always develop these skills.

As a result, accommodation and remediation efforts are available to these children through college. Study guides; note-takers; tutors; books on tape; the use of computerized scanners that can present, highlight, and read any printed material to your child (e.g., Kurzweil Omni 3000; Premier Assistive Technology's Universal Reader); the use of Internet knowledge sites and CD versions of encyclopedias to simplify information searches; the use of word processing software and voice-recognition technology to facilitate writing (e.g., ViaVoice or Dragon's Naturally Speaking); the availability of portable word processing equipment in the classroom (e.g., "DreamWriter," "Alpha Smart," or laptop computers); testing modifications; and homework accommodations are all "permissible" through the college and post-graduate level in the United States.

What is the reason for all this "help"? Specific federal laws! One of the founding principles of our country is the "pursuit of happiness." Federal law specifies that individuals with handicapping conditions cannot be subjected to discrimination. An individual who is unable to read because of dyslexia is entitled to be educated in a manner that accommodates (and if possible, remediates) the disability. However, if this individual is never able to read, he or she should not be prevented from becoming a doctor, lawyer, or any other chosen career simply because his or her educational setting refuses to accommodate the instructional methods. To do so is, quite frankly, in violation of federal law.

How Can I Apply This to My Child?

To begin the process of obtaining help for your child, the child needs to have been diagnosed with ADHD by a qualified health care professional (typically a physician, a licensed clinical social worker, or a psychologist). After your child is diagnosed with ADHD, you'll need to make a written request for an evaluation by your school district's Committee on Special Educational Services (CSE). The letter should be addressed to the chairperson of the CSE. This person is sometimes referred to as the director of Special Education Services or the director of Student Services. While districts may vary the title given to the person responsible for organizing the evaluation, every school district that receives federal or state funds for education must have such a committee and a person responsible for conducting meetings to develop a plan of academic remediation, support, and accommodation (as needed). An example of such a letter is provided here.

Sample Letter to the CSE

Date:

To: Chairperson of the CSE

From: Mr. & Mrs. B.

Re: Timothy B.

Dear _____

My child, Timothy B., was recently evaluated by Dr. Monastra, a licensed psychologist. Based on an extensive review of medical, developmental, academic, and social histories; evaluation of behavioral ratings provided by us and by Timothy's teachers; and psychological assessment of Timothy's attentional abilities, Dr. Monastra diagnosed our child with Attention Deficit Hyperactivity Disorder (ADHD). A copy of Dr. Monastra's report is included with this letter in support of the diagnosis.

As required by federal and state law, we are requesting an evaluation by our school district's Committee for Special Educational Services. It is our understanding that because our child has been diagnosed with ADHD, testing for specific learning disabilities and a functional assessment to determine the ways that our son's ADHD is interfering with school performance are required. We are requesting that both be conducted so that an Individual Educational Plan (IEP) or a 504 Accommodation Plan can be developed, depending on my child's need. A copy of a Functional Assessment Checklist for Teachers is included to aid in the evaluation process.

Thank you for your prompt attention to this request.

Sincerely,

Mr. & Mrs. B.

I strongly recommend that this type of letter be sent by certified mail to whomever is the chairperson of the CSE or the director of Special Educational Services. This individual is required by law to proceed with an evaluation once a written referral is made. I have seen years wasted by parents talking with their child's teachers, guidance counselors, or principal about getting services for their child. Whereas I am in support of consultation among parents, teachers, principals, counselors, and school psychologists for a 6-month period, I do not believe that the best interest of the child is served by delaying referral to the CSE if problems at school persist beyond that time frame. A certified letter ensures that there is no misunderstanding about the timing and nature of the parents' request and the school's legal requirements.

After you have mailed the letter to the school district, you will be contacted and asked to sign a form that permits evaluation by the CSE. You are also likely to be asked to provide the district with information about your child's medical, developmental, and social histories. This information may be obtained through an interview or by asking you to complete detailed questionnaires.

The evaluation at school will include individual testing of your child's intelligence, as well as her or his abilities in the areas of reading decoding, reading comprehension, computation, mathematical reasoning, listening comprehension, and written expression. This testing is typically performed by a school psychologist or a special education teacher. In addition, classroom observation often will be conducted by the school psychologist and questionnaires evaluating your child's behavior in the classroom will be completed by teacher(s). Finally, I request that teachers complete a Functional Assessment Checklist for Teachers (a copy is provided later in this lesson), so that each area of functional impairment can be identified and subsequently addressed in the child's educational plan.

After the evaluations are completed, a meeting will be scheduled by the CSE. Attending this meeting will be the chairperson (who presides over the meeting), the school psychologist, a special education teacher, one of your child's teachers, a parent representative (i.e., a person whose child receives supportive services through your school district), possibly your child's guidance counselor, and, on occasion, the school nurse and the building principal (or principal's designee). You are entitled to be at this meeting and can request that your child's psychologist (or other expert) attend the meeting to assist in developing the educational plan.

One of the most important services a psychologist (or other expert) can provide is attendance at the CSE meeting. Because the psychologist (or other expert) that you bring to the meeting should be knowledgeable about ADHD and educational law, he or she can assist the committee in developing a comprehensive plan that will promote your child's academic success. This expert also can provide you with some much needed support during a meeting that is often overwhelming and intimidating to parents. However, as you participate in the CSE meeting *it is essential to keep in mind that the diagnosis of ADHD qualifies your child for assistance*. Your child's "entitlement" to accommodation or assistance is not a matter for debate. What is "up for discussion" is the type of accommodation or assistance that will be needed to promote your child's success.

During the meeting, each member of the committee will present test results and observations (as will you and any consultants that accompany you). If there is sufficient evidence that your child's health impairment is affecting his or her alertness in school (e.g., doesn't complete assignments in class, is distracted in class, does not take accurate class notes, fails to remember books, forgets homework, doesn't follow directions, takes hours to complete assignments that other kids finish in 15 minutes, is unable to develop and use study guides) and that report card "grades" or other indicators of "educational performance" are adversely affected by this lack of alertness, then your child's ADHD is a health impairment that meets IDEA requirements. The next step is for the committee to develop a plan of remediation, support, and accommodation, depending on the severity of the functional impairment. The district is required to develop a program that addresses each of the child's functional impairments. The CSE will develop a plan that is the "least restrictive" option to ensure that the child can benefit from as many of the programs available in the general educational setting as possible before providing "special education" services. However, if the program that is developed is not promoting your child's success, you can request a meeting to revise the educational plan (IEP or 504 Plan) at any time, by writing to the CSE chairperson.

To help school districts evaluate the type and severity of a student's functional problems, I developed (and copyrighted) The Functional Assessment Checklist for Teachers (FACT). A copy of the FACT is provided on the next page for your use. The purpose of the form is to help teachers and the CSE evaluate functional impairment in a systematic manner so that a comprehensive program can be developed for the child. This form should be distributed to each of your child's teachers and the results shared with your child's psychologist prior to the meeting.

THE FUNCTIONAL ASSESSMENT CHECKLIST FOR TEACHERS

(FACT)

Copyright: Vincent J. Monastra, PhD

Student's Name: _____

Teacher's Name: _____

Date of Rating: _____

Dear: _____

As you are aware, children with ADHD have a health impairment that can adversely affect their functioning at school. To develop comprehensive intervention programs that can promote the success of these children, functional assessment of the child's behavior at school is essential. Your assistance in this process would be greatly appreciated.

The following statements relate to specific abilities that are commonly affected by ADHD. Please read each statement and assign a value using the following scale.

1. Far worse than peers
2. Slightly worse than peers
3. About the same as peers
4. Slightly better than peers
5. Much better than peers
N. Not expected at this age

ORGANIZATION:

_____ arrives to class on time
_____ has necessary materials (textbook, paper, etc.)
_____ brings homework assignments to class

_____ records homework assignments in planner/agenda

_____ brings home the materials necessary to complete homework

CLASSROOM FUNCTIONING:

_____ sits in seat, does not disrupt class with extraneous movements or verbalizations

_____ follows written directions

_____ follows verbal directions

_____ accurately copies notes from chalkboard/overheads

_____ completes "seat work" during the allowed time

_____ takes accurate notes from lectures or instructional presentations

_____ participates appropriately in class discussions (does not interrupt; stays on topic)

SOCIAL SKILLS:

_____ maintains eye contact while speaking;

_____ maintains eye contact while listening

_____ engages in social conversations with peers

_____ is able to maintain a conversation that is of interest to the other person

_____ is invited by peers to join social activities

_____ is involved in school-based extracurricular activities (e.g., sports, music, drama)

AFFECTIVE CONTROL:

_____ tolerates frustration

_____ verbally aggressive with peers

_____ verbally aggressive with staff

_____ complies with rules

_____ physically aggressive with peers

_____ physically aggressive with staff

_____ seems anxious/worried

_____ seems sad/depressed

ACADEMIC SKILLS:

Reading:

_____ reading speed and accuracy
_____ ability to comprehend the content of passages
_____ ability to reach conclusions based on inference
_____ ability to prepare outlines/study guides based on reading of textbook

Mathematics:

_____ knowledge of number facts (addition/subtraction)
_____ knowledge of multiplication facts
_____ computational accuracy
_____ ability to understand "word" problems and calculate the correct answer

Written Expression:

_____ writing speed
_____ writing legibility
_____ spelling skills
_____ grammar skills

_____ ability to write answers requiring a single sentence
_____ ability to write short essays (1 to 2 paragraphs)
_____ ability to write compositions (3+ paragraphs)

During the CSE meeting, the results of the FACT (or another type of assessment tool) need to be reviewed to develop a clear picture of the ways your child's ADHD (and learning disabilities) are interfering with school success. This information serves as the basis for the development of an IEP or 504 Plan. Individual Educational Plans (IEPs) are developed if there appears to be the need for services by special education teachers. 504 Plans are developed if you and the district are of the opinion that your child could be successful without special educational services provided the child is given certain "reasonable" accommodations. A sample of the kinds of accommodations that are considered "reasonable" by at least two school districts (Broward County, Florida; Vestal Central School District, New York) is provided below. Accommodations include modifications in the physical arrangement of the room, lesson presentation, completion of assignments, test taking, organization, and behavioral expectations.

ACCOMMODATIONS PROVIDED IN ACCORDANCE WITH SECTION 504 OF THE REHABILITATION ACT OF 1973

PHYSICAL ARRANGEMENT OF THE ROOM:

_____ seating child near the teacher
_____ seating student near a positive role model
_____ teacher will stand near the student when giving directions or presenting lessons
_____ student will be placed away from distracting stimuli (air conditioner, window, door)
_____ teacher will increase the distance between the student's desk and those of classmates

LESSON PRESENTATION:

_____ pair students to check accuracy of work
_____ write key points on the board
_____ provide peer tutoring
_____ provide visual aides
_____ provide peer note taker
_____ provide written outline
_____ allow student to taperecord lessons
_____ have child review key points orally
_____ use computer-assisted instruction (software, Internet)
_____ permit student to use word processing technology to take notes
_____ make sure directions are understood
_____ include a variety of activities during each lesson
_____ divide longer presentations into shorter segments

ASSIGNMENTS–WORKSHEETS:

_____ give extra time to complete tasks
_____ simplify complex directions

_____ hand out worksheets one at a time

_____ reduce the reading level of the assignments

_____ require fewer correct responses to achieve grade

_____ require fewer repetitions of practice work (e.g., writing spelling words)

_____ reduce the number of homework assignments

_____ allow student to taperecord assignments or homework

_____ allow student to use typewriter, word processor, or computer to complete work

_____ provide structural guides for completing written assignments

_____ provide study skills training

_____ give frequent short quizzes and avoid long tests

_____ shorten assignments; divide work into smaller segments

_____ not grade handwriting or spelling (unless a spelling test)

TEST MODIFICATIONS:

_____ allow extra time to complete test

_____ permit test to be taken in a low distraction context

_____ permit use of assistive technology (tape recorder, computer, word processor, or typewriter) to record answers

_____ read test items to the student

_____ read directions to the student; check to determine understanding of directions

_____ give exam orally

_____ give take-home tests

_____ use more objective questions (fewer essay responses)

_____ give frequent short quizzes, not long exams

_____ allow periodic "breaks" during testing

_____ allow periodic interaction with teacher or examiner to promote attention to task

ORGANIZATION:

_____ provide peer assistance with organizational skills

_____ assign homework buddy

_____ provide extra set of books at home

_____ send daily or weekly progress reports home, listing specific assignments that were not completed or returned and defining any behavioral concerns

_____ develop a reward system for classroom work and homework completion

_____ provide student with a homework assignment notebook

_____ check accuracy of daily assignment notebook

_____ prompt student regarding assignments and materials that need to be brought home

_____ prompt student in the morning to turn in completed homework

BEHAVIOR:

_____ develop and implement a classroom behavior management system

_____ praise specific behaviors

_____ use privileges and rewards for specific behaviors

_____ make "prudent use" of negative consequences

_____ keep classroom rules simple and clear

_____ allow for short breaks between assignments

_____ use non-verbal cues to help student stay on task

_____ mark student's correct answers, not mistakes

_____ permit time out of seat for "movement" (e.g., run errands)

_____ allow movement that does not distract others

_____ develop "contracts" with the student

_____ use time-out procedures

_____ ignore inappropriate behaviors not drastically outside classroom limits

Like the FACT, this list of accommodations should be available at the time of your CSE meeting. It is intended to be used as a reference by you and the committee. The goal of the committee is to develop a plan that includes (as needed) instruction by a special education teacher and provision for certain types of accommodations and modifications designed to help your child succeed. Once you and your district are in agreement regarding the plan, a written version of the plan will be submitted to the Board of Education in your school district. Once accepted, the provisions in the plan must be followed. Educational law requires that these plans must be reviewed (and revised if necessary) at least once per year. In addition, should the plan need revision before the year is completed, it can be revised at the written request of the parent or the school.

Homework

A lot of information was presented to you in this lesson. Before you proceed to the next lesson, take a little time to think about how your child is doing in school. If your son or daughter has ADHD, do they have an IEP or 504 Plan? How is it working? If they are a student of "average" intelligence, are they obtaining marks of Bs and Cs on their report cards? If they are considered to be of "above average" or "superior" intelligence, are they on the honor roll? If so, great. If not, revision is needed.

The purpose of educational laws is to make sure that your child is succeeding at school, demonstrating an ability to learn academic material at a level consistent with his or her intelligence. If your child of above average intelligence is receiving grades of 65 to 70 because he or she is not completing (or is forgetting to turn in) assignments, the IEP needs to be revised. If your child is failing courses because she or he cannot prepare study guides, the IEP needs to be revised. If your child is being repeatedly disciplined for ADHD behaviors (e.g., unable to complete seat work "on time"; failure to return homework assignments; speaking out of turn; displaying restlessness while seated), the IEP needs to be revised. Write to the CSE chairperson and get the process started.

Similarly, if your child has been diagnosed with ADHD but is not receiving academic support, now is the time to write a letter to your district's CSE chairperson. While efforts to motivate students through rewards and punishments are understandable, it is a gross mistake to believe that such strategies alone will overcome the range of functional impairments caused by ADHD. Kids with ADHD need an educational plan that specifically targets their multiple areas of functional impairment. Whereas use of daily and weekly feedback from teachers to parents can help increase student motivation, anyone who understands that ADHD is a health impairment fully recognizes that such reporting of failure does not breed academic success.

We would not expect a blind child to improve his or her eyesight by withholding privileges or administering punishments. The same holds true for children with other types of health problems, like ADHD. Don't succumb to the notion that the cause of your child's failure is that she or he is hopelessly unmotivated, depressed, or defiant. Don't give away your child's educational rights. Get your child the help he or she deserves.

6

Kids Need a Reason to Learn

During the first five lessons, I spent a lot of time telling you that ADHD is a medical condition, that it is inherited, and that at least some of the symptoms are likely to continue into adulthood. You've read about how medications for ADHD work and how proper nutrition can help your child. However, even though medication and dietary changes can help your child's brain "wake up," many problems at home and school will continue without systematic intervention.

Sometimes I think that medicines for ADHD help in the same way that a medicine for blindness might. What I mean is this. Let's say that someone developed a medicine that cured blindness. After a patient took the medicine, he or she would be able to see. However, she or he wouldn't know the names of numerous objects that could now be seen. The patient wouldn't know how to read printed words or how to "read" facial expressions (among other things).

A similar type of process occurs with ADHD. When a patient is treated with an effective dose of medication, the patient often feels that he or she can sit still, pay attention, and concentrate for longer periods of time. However, the medicine does not teach the patient how to take notes in class, search books for facts, prepare study guides, complete outlines and essays, or study for tests. The medicine does not develop a plan so the patient is organized and remembers important aspects of life. The medicine does not create an ability to find the words needed to have conversations that are of interest to other kids (or his or her parents). The medicine does not help a child know how to solve problems that occur at home, at school, or in the neighborhood. That kind of knowledge must be taught and learned.

Earlier in this book, I provided you with a long list of lessons that you might want your child to learn. The lessons listed in "Dr. Monastra's Top Forty" are those that commonly need to be taught to children with ADHD. Take a few moments to look at that list. As you look at it, remember that some of the lessons will be addressed at school, through the development of an Individual Education Plan or 504 Accommodation Plan. However, other skills will need to be developed primarily at home. In this lesson, I examine how you can help your child overcome some of the social and academic problems that are part of ADHD.

How Do Kids Learn New Skills?

A fair amount is known about the learning process. Here are some basics:

1. *The "teacher" (in this case, you) needs to select a skill that the child is physically able to learn.* For example, you might be able to teach a 6-year-old to organize his or her belongings by picking up toys after playing. You would not be successful if you asked the same child to organize the garage. So the first question you need to ask yourself when you think about teaching your child is, "Are other kids (within a year or two of your child's age) able to perform the skill that I am trying to teach?"

2. *The child needs to be attending when you are teaching.* This means that to teach your child to learn, you need to make sure that he or she is listening (and looking if you are showing the child something). Because kids with ADHD often listen while looking at other things, this doesn't mean that you have to get into an argument over "looking" at you. It just means that you need to check and make sure the child heard you.

3. *Your lesson needs to be brief and to the point.* If you make a big preliminary speech about your child's laziness and how frustrated you are and then launch into your directions, chances are that your kid has drifted off. If you want your child to pick up all clothes, toys, books, and food wrappers from the floor of his or her room and put them in a box (for later sorting), then tell the child that. Kids with ADHD do not have an internalized model of what a clean bedroom looks like. They need to learn. Similarly, if your child needs to study for a test, it is pointless to tell the child to

"Go to your room and study." The kid probably has no idea how to study. Again, you'll need to teach your child or hire a tutor to help him or her learn how to study (e.g., "Let's look at your chapter review. I'll ask you the questions. If there is any question you can't answer, I'll help you find the information and write the answer down on a piece of paper or index card. You can memorize the facts on each card, and I'll test you to make sure that you know most of them").

4. *The child needs to have a reason for learning.* This is a biggie. Without "motivation" there is little learning. Think back to your high school or college days. If a teacher told you to read a book chapter or a magazine article before the next class, did you always do it? If my memory is working, I remember that there was always someone in the class who'd ask, "Is this going to be on the test?" or "Are we going to have a quiz on this?" If the teacher said, "Yes," chances are you'd try to read it. If the teacher said, "No," chances are you wouldn't. Now there was always the chance that you were absolutely fascinated by the subject matter (a long shot for most of us) and would read the material because you were interested in it. However, without that type of interest, most of us needed some type of external motivator (e.g., the knowledge that we'd be grounded, lose our driving privileges, or be unable to play sports for our school team).

Let's try to apply that memory to teaching the child with ADHD. It is true that your child will need some type of motivating reason to learn and do what he or she has been taught. However, unlike kids without ADHD, it is important for you to realize that some long-term reward, like a special trip, or "punishment" like being grounded or being dropped from the football team, is not going to work. It is highly unlikely that your child will get all passing grades, turn in all assignments, and not have a single disciplinary referral simply because you offered to take the child to Disney World as reward for that kind of effort over a 10-week marking period. It is equally unlikely that a major turnaround would occur if you grounded your child for days or weeks if the child did not pass a test, turn in an assignment, or got into trouble at school.

I encourage parents not to use such a "big bang" approach. Instead, I want you to think about all the "free" pleasures that your child receives every day. Many kids get to watch cable television and have access to literally hundreds of channels. Others are able to play incredibly fascinating video games on computers or their Nintendos, PlayStations, X-boxes, or GameCubes. They often are able to explore an incredible world of information and communication "online." They can go outside and ride their bikes; rollerblade; skateboard; or play soccer, baseball, basketball, football, or other sports. They can build with their Legos. They can play the guitar, the piano, the drums, or other instruments. They can go to karate, scouts, and participate as a member of a sporting team. Instead of offering your kids money, a "big event," or some other "all or nothing" type of deal, I want you to begin thinking about how you can use these daily pleasures to motivate your child to learn.

For example, let's say you want your child to learn to keep the floor of the bedroom free of toys, clothing, papers, food, and drinks. You've told your son or daughter to keep the room "picked up" hundreds of times. It's morning. You wake up and battle to get your child awake, fed, washed, dressed, and out the door. For reasons unknown to you or me, you walk into the bedroom as the child is getting ready. You notice that the room is a mess. You hit the roof. You tell your child that because he or she didn't pick up, he or she is grounded after school. What is likely to happen now? Big emotional meltdown!

What about after school? Well, there is little chance that your child will ground him- or herself (because you're working). And because on the schedule that night is one of the twice-weekly soccer league games (and we can't let the team down), the kid gets to play soccer. So even though you've told your child to pick up the bedroom hundreds of times, made sure you had her or his attention when you said it, and had even shown the child what a clean room looks like, there is no reason for your child to do what you've asked. After all, the child was able to come home after school, have a snack, watch television, play video games, talk with friends, and maybe even get homework done (a long shot). To top it off, tonight there is a game. The child may think, "why pick up my room?" (even if he or she somehow remembers the need to do so).

An essential truth to keep in mind is that your child is unlikely to be inspired to do what you want because of some internalized motivational source (e.g., "It will make Mom happy"; "I've got to learn to be organized so I can be successful when I go to Harvard"). Without an immediate, concrete reason that can't be ignored, you'll harp on the same issue forever. My suggestion for the kid with the messy room is some variation of the following: "Billy, after school you'll need to pick up the toys, clothes, and junk off the floor and put them in this bag before you can go to soccer. If the room is not picked up by the time I get home, you'll have that job, plus another one to do. We'll go to soccer when they're both done. So it's up to you, son." The key element here is that the child needs to comply with your requests to earn the right to do something that she or he has been getting for free. A lesson I share with my patients with ADHD is that their parents are trying to help them grow up. When they were babies, everything was free. Now that they are growing up and want to do "big kid" stuff, they have to earn it. *In life, you get what you work for.* Moms and dads need to help kids learn that lesson.

The other thing you need to keep in mind is that you don't have to bribe your kid with toys, trips to the mall, videos, video games, or money to motivate them to learn the lessons you are trying to teach. Instead, as you think about your child's day and all the "freebies" he or she receives regardless of whether the child listens to you or not, you'll come to realize that there is a world of opportunity to use those types of activities to "inspire" better effort. Instead of bribing, I will examine ways to organize your household so your child needs to earn life's daily pleasures. There are very few freebies and no "sacred cows" (not even little league baseball games). In the next lesson I talk about the systematic use of daily pleasures to motivate and the use of a procedure I call "Time Stands Still." More on that in a little bit.

5. *Kids learn best from teachers who are respectful and show that they care.* Before I discuss strategies like "Time Stands Still" and the use of daily pleasures, I want to take a minute to emphasize one last piece in the learning process. It has to do with the characteristics of the "teacher." Think back on your childhood. Whom do you remember as an effective teacher? For many people, a somewhat demanding teacher who was firm but fair may come to mind. This person may not have had a great sense of humor. Probably, the teacher gave you a lot of homework. But there was something about this teacher that made you work a little harder. Maybe you had the sense that he or she liked or respected you. Maybe this teacher spoke with you about your ability. Maybe the teacher took a little time after class to explain lessons to you. Maybe she or he had a kind word for you when the teacher saw you in the hall. Maybe this teacher took an interest in your activities.

The bottom line is you had the sense that this teacher cared about you. And you responded. This type of teacher model can be quite useful in teaching kids with ADHD, whether at school or at home.

Other effective teachers have a great sense of humor and can teach very complex ideas in enjoyable ways. These teachers are highly creative and fun. They hold the attention of students because they are entertaining. Just like the preacher who cracks a few jokes, these teachers help kids learn because most people pay closer attention after a refreshing bit of humor. If you have a good sense of humor and can find the fun in teaching mundane things like brushing teeth or picking up a room, you might be able to use this type of teaching strategy.

A third type of teaching style uses a lot of criticism, threats, and punishment. When a child makes a mistake, forgets, or fails to comply with a parental request, she or he is spoken to harshly, "put down," and receives some type of punishment (e.g., a restriction to the bedroom for the remainder of the day or the loss of a planned activity). Believe it or not, I have even interviewed kids who have told me that they "lost Christmas" because their rooms were a mess and they were fighting with their brothers and sisters too much. In these families, the parents threw out the Christmas presents in an effort to teach their children to obey. Although the memory of the loss of Christmas remained a disturbing one to these children, the parents' use of this harsh approach failed to stop the fighting or get the rooms clean. Remember, regardless of how severely a parent (or teacher) criticizes or punishes a child with ADHD, such punitive approaches fail miserably with these children. Instead, children with ADHD seem to become increasingly aggressive in response to this type of approach.

As your child's primary teacher when it comes to learning those personal skills needed to succeed in life, it is up to you to decide what type of teacher you will be. For the most part, I think people in general tend to learn more from someone we feel cares about us and respects us. The same is true with our kids. Each child needs to know that his or her parents (or other caregivers) love him or her and think that their child is an "okay" person. It will be important for you to communicate that to your child, day to day, as you work on teaching new skills.

HOMEWORK

During the coming week, I want you to begin thinking about a couple of topics. First, I want you to consider the amount of time that you get to spend saying or doing something "nice" with your kid. Here's what I mean by "nice." For at least 15 minutes each day, I'd like you to be in a room with your child and actually interact with them (talking, "hanging out," or doing something) without asking questions, giving directions, or correcting them. Now this may sound very simple, but check out what happens most times you are near your child. Chances are that you ask questions, tell your child to do something, or to stop doing something. I am asking you to be in the same room without doing any of that, at least once a day, every day, for 15 minutes. That's what I mean by nice.

The reason this is important is that by the time many ADHD kids get to the age of 8 years, they start to react to your presence with indifference or a bit of dread. If the only time that your child hears you call his or her name is when he or she is in trouble or needs to do some kind of chore, why listen? Letting your child know that you are interested in being with him or her for reasons other than "bossing around" is a good place to start. Your child needs to feel that you actually like being her or his parent, that you love and want to be with your child, and that your child is more than just a burden to you.

The second task has to do with taking a closer look at the reasons your child continues to do things that you want her or him to stop (or fails to do the tasks you want the child to start). Pull out your "Top 40" list. Select around six lessons that you want your child to learn. Write each down on a separate piece of paper. Now do the following:

Think about what it takes for a child to learn. For each of the lessons that you have been trying to teach your child, ask yourself the following:

1. Am I looking for my kid to do something beyond his or her years (within two years of his or her age)?
2. Do I have my child's attention when I'm trying to teach?
3. Have I shown my child what I want her or him to do (or stop doing)?
4. Is there a reason for my child to do what I want?
5. Am I speaking to my son or daughter in a way that demonstrates caring?

As you think about those lessons that your child has not yet "learned," you'll probably find that some of the reasons are found in the answers to these questions. Another common reason for feeling as though you have "failed as a parent" is because there are so many things going wrong that you don't know where to start. I help you with that as we go through these lessons. For now, just begin to think about the kinds of lessons that you want to teach and the importance of developing a specific plan. In the next few lessons, I talk specifically about ways to help your child become more organized, able to complete responsibilities, learn behavioral and emotional control, and develop effective problem-solving skills. To help you begin this process, I include a guide for you to use.

GUIDE FOR TEACHING SKILLS TO YOUR CHILD

1. Write down one lesson that you want to teach your child.

   _____

   _____

2. Is this something that kids 2 years younger are able to do? _____

   If no, pick another lesson.

3. When are you going to do your "teaching"?

   _____

   Pick a time and place with few distractions.

4. Have you told or shown your child what you wanted him or her to do (or stop doing)?

   _____

5. What will happen if your child does what you want?

   _____

   _____

   Make sure that the child knows this.

6. What will happen if your child doesn't do what you want?

   _____

   _____

   Make sure that the child knows this.

7

You'll Get Lost Without a Lesson Plan

As I begin parenting classes at my clinic, I am often struck by how tired and drained the parents of my patients look. I treat a wide range of patients, from 4-year-old children to adults in their 70s. However, most of my patients are school-age children. This means that most of my parents have had to essentially function as their child's frontal lobe for over a decade. They needed to remain highly vigilant to help their child fulfill responsibilities. They had to be ever mindful of their child's whereabouts to protect the child from harm. They spent hours calming their child when the child was uncontrollably distraught over events that others would shrug off. They exhausted themselves as they tried to convince their child not to act on aggressive impulses when frustrated. By the time they see me, they have tried pretty much everything that others have suggested. And they are tired and frustrated.

As this book follows the outline of the program in use at my clinic, you and I are now seven sessions into the book (or "class"). We still haven't set up a single "token economy" (a home program where kids earn points or chips to buy fun time or rewards). There are no "star charts" plastered on the refrigerator door. The kids are not receiving stickers, dimes, or dollars for each "good behavior." And yet, you parents are beginning to look a bit more energized. The reason? Some very significant events have occurred.

For example, if you are following my plan, your child has been evaluated by a physician to make sure she or he does not have any other medical problem that can cause symptoms of inattention, hyperactivity, and impulsivity. Approximately 5% of children have been diagnosed with other medical problems that have been contributing to these symptoms (most commonly, allergies, hypoglycemia, and psychoactive substance abuse), and treatments for these problems have been initiated. Nutritional evaluations are complete and dietary problems identified. Efforts to improve your child's diet have likewise begun. As most of my patients are treated with medication for ADHD, I expect your child's physician also has taken steps to identify an effective type and dose of medication and that your child is beginning to respond.

In addition, parents should have written letters to the chairpersons of their school districts' committee for special education. If so, educational evaluations are now in process at school for the child. Some children may have started to receive academic support at this time. At home, parents are trying to spend some "play" time with their children. In short, you have begun to set the stage for teaching at home.

In some ways, I compare initial efforts at my clinic to work in an emergency room. The patient comes in, there is a great degree of risk, and the first task is to stabilize the patient's medical condition. This is what we have done so far: stabilized the situation so you can begin to teach your child some important skills. It is time to develop your lesson plans.

PARENTS AS TEACHERS

As I mentioned before, my hope is that you can fight the tendency to get overwhelmed by the number of lessons that you want to teach your child. Parenting requires a lesson plan. Like any other teacher, you need to realize that you should teach one lesson at a time. I encourage my parents to remember that there are 52 weeks in a year. That means that if you only teach one lesson each week, you will have taught 52 lessons that year. However, to be honest, I haven't been involved in too many situations in which the number of significant problems exceeded a dozen or so. By the time parents are comfortable with the idea of systematically using daily pleasures to motivate and have experienced success with the first six lessons, teaching begins to move forward with much less effort. So, as we continue with your lesson plan, it is important to realize that it is better to work on a few lessons at a time and to remember that your child will need a reason to learn. This will be as true for the other children in your family as for your child with ADHD.

When parents consider ways to motivate their children with ADHD, the use of "reinforcers" (e.g., "objects" like money, toys, or videos, or "activities" like playing outside, visiting a friend, use of the family computer or computer games) typically comes to mind. However, parents and counselors who treat children with ADHD have learned that it isn't easy to use objects or activities to motivate kids with ADHD to complete daily tasks like getting up in the morning; eating a nutritious breakfast; brushing teeth; getting dressed; making it out the door to catch the school bus on time; cooperating with the teacher; completing assigned work; bringing home and completing homework; listening to (and doing) what mom and dad ask them to do; getting along with brothers and sisters; helping with chores like cleaning their room or other areas in the house; and getting to bed without a fight. Unlike other kids (who might have little problem completing 90% of these tasks), kids with ADHD need "motivation" to complete nearly all of these tasks.

If your child doesn't have ADHD and does 90% of these tasks anyway (but leaves his or her room a mess), then you could easily use a reinforcer like "not going out after school to play until the room is cleaned" to inspire the child. The child who does not have ADHD would most likely come home and quickly put her or his clothes in drawers (or closet), pick up trash off the floor, and put toys in some type of container or on a shelf. Now, I'm not saying the job would be done perfectly. However, those areas needing further work (e.g., the closet where everything was piled into) could be pointed out and the child informed that the closet also needed to be organized. Although the kid without ADHD would not be too happy about the parent's actions, it is highly unlikely that the child would have a meltdown and trash the room. A kid with ADHD might.

Let's look at how this "room cleaning" requirement would work for the kid with ADHD. The child comes home but probably forgets that he or she needs to clean the room. If you are home, you'll need to remind the child, because odds are he or she is already playing. So, you have to interrupt playtime (and listen to the arguing and pleading) and direct the child to go clean up. More debate and arguing is likely to come next. Finally, when the child gets to the bedroom, she or he will probably get distracted and start playing with something else. Old toys, pieces of paper, and other memorabilia can be quite fascinating when the alternative is to begin putting away clothes, toys, or other things.

After a half hour or so of thinking that your child is busily cleaning the room, you check in on the child to discover that nothing has happened. So, you remind the child to get started or he or she can't go outside to play. However, by now it's getting dark anyway. So maybe you threaten that the child won't be able to go out tomorrow. Or maybe you threaten to ground your child from television or video games. Regardless of what you do, this is a hopeless situation that is going nowhere fast. And this is only one of the numerous tasks that you want your child to complete on a daily basis.

Because doctors and counselors have long recognized that children with ADHD do not usually respond well to the kind of reinforcers typically used by parents, more systematic approaches have been developed. One involves the development of home behavior charts or programs (sometimes called Point Systems, Star Charts, or Token Economies) that chart the specific kinds of tasks the child is expected to complete and the specific kinds of objects and activities that he or she can earn by completing them. If the child completes the desired task (e.g., doing homework), or acts in certain desired ways (e.g., not arguing, playing cooperatively), he or she can earn a reward (e.g., money or a toy) or permission to do some activity (e.g., play a video game or visit a friend). If the child does not complete the task or act in the desired way, he or she does not earn the reward. Such programs have been studied for some time and, when well thought out, can be helpful in promoting the development of children with ADHD.

However, because many parents I work with have ADHD themselves or are overwhelmed by the prospects of developing a comprehensive home charting plan, it is often easier to use a simpler "Work for Play" type of program. In the Work for Play program, the day is divided into four time periods (before school, at school, before dinner, after dinner). The child needs to complete certain tasks to earn the privilege to engage in any recreational activity during each time period.

In Work for Play, if the child does what is required, he or she can play for that time period. If the child does not do what is required, a procedure called "Time Stands Still" is used. In this process, the child does not have permission to engage in any activity other than the one required by the parent. His or her life is "on hold" until the child complies. The more time the child delays (and defies his or her parents or says upsetting things), the more the child will need to do to make up for these actions.

This process is quite different from Time Out because there is no time limit on the "punishment." In Time Stands Still, the child needs to comply with parental requests and make up for disrespectful actions before he or she can play. This is intended to place responsibility clearly on the child's shoulders and to teach the lesson that people need to apologize and make amends when they do things that upset or hurt others.

If the child defies and plays anyway (without permission), she or he will need to apologize, do some type of corrective activity (to make up), and obey the parent's request. If the defiance occurs before school, the child cannot play after school until she or he apologizes, does some type of corrective activity, and complies with parental requests. Let's take a few minutes and see how each approach works.

Home Behavioral Charts

Most parents who attend my classes have heard something about using charts in teaching children with ADHD. Sometimes the words "Token Economy" are used. Sometimes these charts will be called "Point Systems" or "Star Charts." Dr. Harvey Parker, a specialist in creating such programs, uses the term "home behavior chart" and publishes a manual to help parents create these plans (Specialty Press, Inc., 300 NW 70th Avenue, Plantation, FL 33317; phone: 305-792-8944). Let me show you a sample program published by Dr. Parker. It describes the skills that Mr. and Mrs. Jones would like their son, Robert, to "Start," as well as the behaviors that these parents want their son to "Stop." Reasons for "learning" these parental lessons are listed as "Rewards." Let's take a look at Robert's chart.

Looking at Robert's Home Behavior Chart, his parents wanted their son to wake up by 7:30 a.m., walk the dog, put his school books back in his bag, clean his bedroom, do his homework, brush his teeth, and jot down notes if he answered the phone. They would award him "points" for any test or paper returned with a grade of "A" or "B" and give "bonus" points for completed "term papers." Hardly unreasonable re-

Robert's Home Behavior Chart

START		VALUE	SUN.	MON.	TUES.	WED.	THURS.	FRI.	SAT.
WAKES	7:30	2		2		2	2	2	
WALKS	DOG	2		2		2	2	2	2
BOOKS	IN BAG	1		1	1		1	1	1
CLEAN	BEDRM	2		2	2	2		2	2
HOME	WORK	3	3	3	3	3	3		3
BRUSH	TEETH	1@	3	2	3	3	3	3	3
WRITE	NOTES	1	1	1		1	1		1
MARKS	A OR B	2		2	2		2	2	
BONUS	PAPER	10							
	TOTAL		7	15	11	13	14	12	12
STOP BEHAVIORS									
BUTTS	IN	–5	–5						–5
YELLS		–5		–5					
FIGHT		–10							
TAKES	STUFF	–10							
HOME	LATE	–10			–10				
LEAVE	HOUSE	–10							
	TOTAL		–5	–5		–10			–5
ROBERT EARNS			2	10	11	3	14	12	2
REWARDS		COST							
GAME	30MIN	3		3	3	3		3	3
T.V.	30MIN	3		3	3	3		3	6
PLAY	OUTSIDE	3							
STAY UP LATER		4							4
SWEET	SNACK	3			3				
BUY	CARDS	10							
SLEEP	OVER	20							
BUY	CD	30							
	USED		0	6	9	6	10	6	13
	LEFT		2	6	8	5	9	15	9

quests. His folks also wanted him to stop butting in, yelling in the house, fighting, taking stuff without asking permission, coming home late, and leaving the house without permission. Also pretty typical requests. To inspire Robert to learn these skills, his parents were offering typical types of rewards and privileges, such as video game time, television time, the privilege of going outside, staying up later, sleeping over with friends, and certain purchases (e.g., CDs or baseball cards). So how did Robert do?

Well on Sunday, he earned a total of 7 points but lost 5 for butting in, which means that he could "buy" none of the available rewards. Now this could be a major problem. I'm sure you've tried preventing your child from enjoying television, video games, or playing outside. That creates a war zone in your house. In addition, once the child knows there is nothing he or she can do to earn what he or she wants, the child has much less of a reason to do what you want. So if you choose to use a Behavior Chart, you need to think of ways for your child to "Get out of Jail," so to speak. For example, on your chart you might want to have a "Start Behavior" called "Makes up" or "Makes Amends." I like to have these in home programs because it means that the child has a chance to earn some privilege by apologizing and doing some type of action to make amends. I'm big on saying, "If you mess up . . . you need to make up."

Now let's look at how Robert did on Monday. Looks like a much better day. He earned 15 points but lost 5 for yelling, which left 10 to spend. He chose to play a video game for 30 minutes and watch television for 30 minutes. Sounds like a nice day on paper, until reality sets in. Have you ever tried to stop a kid who was playing a video game after only one half-hour? Maybe I'm living in a really warped part of the world, but the kids who come into my clinic are none too happy if they have to stop playing a game after 30 minutes. They ignore their parents and keep playing. They plead, beg, whine, or throw a tantrum. If Robert did that, he'd lose 5 points for yelling, 5 more for fighting, and quickly be in the hole.

So on a day in which Robert did pretty much everything his folks wanted (woke up, walked the dog, picked up his books, cleaned his room, did his homework, brushed his teeth twice, jotted down notes, and received "A" or "B" on a school paper), he ended up pretty frustrated and probably in a bit of trouble with his folks. For all his efforts, he was only able to play a video game for 30 minutes, and watch television for 30 minutes. Most kids with ADHD get to do that anyway. To top it off, he probably got angry with his parents when they told him to stop playing his video game. What could be done to make this work out better for Robert and his parents?

One of the most important parts of setting up a home behavioral chart or Token Economy is to run some simulations of how your "new world" is going to play out. On paper, Robert's program looks pretty good. Not too many lessons to be learned. Nice things to earn. Clearly laid out.

Now run some simulations. In the world created by Robert's parents, Robert needs to earn 3 points to watch television or play a video game for 30 minutes. Okay. Let's say he's a bear to wake up, refuses to walk the dog, fails to pick up his books (you grab them from the four corners of the house), and leaves his room a mess. But . . . he brushes his teeth twice (2 points), gets a "B" on last night's math homework (2 points), and does his homework tonight (3 points). He earns 7 points and gets an hour's worth of play. How does that sound to you? Probably not too good. To me, as Robert's doctor, I'm not happy either. In his parents' program, he can basically ignore many of their rules and still end up the day doing what he likes. Not a good outcome.

If I revised this program, I would add a "Start Behavior" like "does what mom or dad asks the first time" (offering 1 to 2 points per time). In fact, that's a mainstay in almost every home behavior chart I work on. I'd also add, "ignores or refuses a mom or dad request" to the "Stop Behaviors" (docking the child 5 to 10 points each time). One other Start Behavior that I'd add is "apologizes and makes up" (earning 1 to 3 points), to give the child a chance to get back into the reward game.

A final recommendation is the elimination of the "carry over" option. As you look at Robert's program, his parents are allowing their son to save points and use them another day. When I use these types of programs, I require kids to use all of their points each day. That way, parents won't get into the situation in which the child has saved enough points to be able to do many fun things while still ignoring their rules.

If a parent would still like to motivate their child by offering a weekly "big ticket item" (like a sleep over or a trip to the movies), they can set weekly targets. For example, if a child could earn a total of 100 points for the school week (5 days), then the child would qualify for a weekend reward on the basis of this effort. I use 90% (90 points) as an "A" effort week that can earn a top quality reward (e.g., overnight at a friend's house; $5–$10 allowance); 80% to 89% (B) earns a lesser quality reward (e.g., video rental; video game rental).

My experience in using home behavior charts is that they can be helpful if they are well thought out. That's why I encourage you to do some dry runs of your program before you put it into action. Otherwise, it can be a disaster. Here is one of my more memorable disaster stories.

I was working with a family who had two children diagnosed with ADHD. Just like Robert's folks, they had a list of "Start Behaviors" (pick up, do chores, complete homework, and so on) and used a variety of "rewards" (game time, television time, play outside, etc.). One of their rewards involved the use of money (the kids could earn $1.00 per point . . . these folks had some serious bucks!). Anyway, of all the things that they wanted their boys to do, the most important was to "get along" and not fight. They really, really, really wanted their sons to stop fighting. And so, the most valued "Start Behavior" was "gets along with brother" (meaning no physical fighting or teasing). The boys could earn 25 points per day for simply not fighting. Guess what happened?

After a couple of days, the boys woke up to the realization that they could basically ignore their parents as long as they just made sure they didn't fight in front of their parents. So they'd earn their 25 points for not fighting, cash it in for money and the right to go outside and do their fighting (as needed) away from home. They'd also politely tell their parents that they really didn't feel like doing their chores or homework and remind them that they still planned on watching television because they had earned it by not fighting. Needless to say, this program was changed pretty quickly.

It is important to realize that when you start one of these programs, you are creating a kind of "bartering program" or "economy" in your home. Take a moment to think about what the rules are in your home. What does your child need to do to earn television time, or video game time, or the right to go to soccer practice, or play outside? Anything? For many families I work with, the child is so impulsive, hyperactive, and emotionally explosive that the parents shy away from confrontation with the child. In those homes, the child gets hundreds of reminders and prompts during the day, the parents spend hours debating to get their child to cooperate and in the end still allow the child to play, watch television, or go to their sporting or other events. If children are to learn the lessons they need to succeed in life, they need to learn that in life we get what we earn. There are no free rides. So, if they want to play outside, watch television, or go to their event after school, they need to earn it, either by doing what they are supposed to do or by making efforts to make amends if they have messed up.

In a similar manner, I work with a number of parents who provide a very rich environment for their child. The child has her or his own television set, with a VCR and a video game system set up in the bedroom. The child might have access to a computer with Internet connection and can visit with friends as he or she talks on his or her personal phone ("Mom, everyone has Road Runner!"). The child plays on a soccer team, attends karate, takes music lessons, and is active in 4-H clubs. Now, these parents can try to motivate their child by saying "Okay, no television or video games tonight." But, if tonight we go to Mickie D's for dinner (because it's "soccer night"), then I play soccer with my buddies, then we get a soda and snack at the refreshment stand because I'm so exhausted from my practice, and then I go home and crash in bed and read my favorite fantasy book . . . who cares if I missed out on TV, I wasn't going to be able to watch it anyway.

If you decide to use a charting type of program, try to minimize the number of "sacred cows." I define a sacred cow activity as one that the child gets to do regardless of his or her actions. My recommendation is that parents eliminate the sacred cow concept. I usually get some tough looks from the fathers in the parenting class who are little league coaches. They tell me that their child has a responsibility to his teammates and can't let them down. I'm not suggesting that you ground your child from "the big game" because he didn't clean up his room, forgot to walk the dog, or yelled at his brother. What I am recommending is that if your child did that, then the child needs to earn the right to play ball by doing some kind of corrective action before the game. Being attentive to that part of the process is an essential ingredient in making Home Behavior Programs successful.

This Sounds Too Complicated to Me ...
Isn't There a Simpler Way?

Yes! As I suggest, charting strategies have a lot of positive ingredients. Parents clearly define what they want their children to learn. Children are informed about the program and know what they need to do and what they can earn. Rewards and privileges are clearly spelled out so kids have a reason to learn the lessons their parents are trying to teach. However, the most glaring problem with these programs is that they can be overwhelming to those parents who have attention deficits themselves. In my classes many, if not most, of the people attending have organizational problems. The charting approach simply overwhelms them.

Let's go back to Robert's chart. His folks wanted him to do certain tasks and stop other behaviors. They created a point system and used that to motivate him. However, their plan required real diligence, a record-keeping system, and a lot of detail. A simpler approach is the Work for Play Plan.

What Do You Mean by Work for Play?

A long time ago, when I was growing up in the suburbs of Philadelphia, I lived on a dead-end street that contained about 50 row homes (the current term is "townhouse"). The houses were all connected. In fact, at night we could talk with our buddies next door through the air vents. There were seemingly hundreds of kids playing on my one block. It was great! And highly motivating. Parents in my neighborhood weren't using point charts or star charts. They used a variation of the Work for Play plan. I'll give you a sample.

Like Robert, kids whose parents were using the Work for Play plan had morning chores and responsibilities. They had to wake up, get washed, dressed, pick up their room, grab breakfast, and be ready for school on time. If they did, great! The child would get a little time to watch television. When the child came home after school, he or she would have some type of simple chore and quickly head out to play (or to watch television).

However, if you gave your mom a hard time and didn't do what you needed to do, there was no morning television. When you came home from school, you did the morning chores that you had failed to do, then you did your after school chore, plus some extra duties (e.g., dusting, cleaning a bathroom, and so on), and then you could go outside or watch television. You needed to be home on time for dinner (or homework). Finally, each child had responsibilities after dinner (e.g., homework, washing dishes, getting ready for bed) before she or he could watch television or play games.

This type of approach created an unspoken kind of organization. The child had certain responsibilities that needed to be finished before the child could earn the rewards or privileges available at that time of day. To earn play time, the child had certain tasks. If the child didn't complete them, she or he was given extra tasks that needed to be completed, in addition to what the child failed to do, before play time could begin. The process included a morning routine, a during-school routine, an after-school routine, and an evening routine. Instead of creating a situation in which the child was grounded or was unable to earn play time because he or she was "bad" in the morning, the child needed to correct the behavior, do what was required, and then make up for the misbehavior by apologizing and doing extra tasks.

The simplicity of this type of plan is often attractive to the parents in my class. It also is easy to implement if your child goes to a child care location after school. As with the charting approach, parents are asked to select goals from the "Dr. Monastra's Top 40" list. The next step is dividing these goals into morning, during school, after school and evening periods and deciding which activities the child gets to earn during each part of the day.

What if My Child Refuses to Do What I Ask?

A common event for parents of kids with ADHD is the emotional upheaval that occurs when the child is asked to do something that the child does not want to do. This could be a chore, homework, or making up for misbehavior. Battle lines will be drawn quickly. The child may start yelling, kicking, throwing things, running out of the room, pounding on walls, and so on. The parent initially tries to be reasonable but eventually resorts to threats and punishments. In these situations, I encourage parents to use something called "Time Stands Still."

Time Stands Still is different from grounding or other types of punishments. It can be used with children from preschool through high school ages. It requires that the child do what was requested by the parent before the child can earn any privilege (or enjoyable activity). Until the child complies with the request, his or her life is on hold. *Time Stands Still.* Or, as I say to my older teenage patients, "You go up to the ATM machine and the machine won't give you any money until you enter the correct code. In this case, the correct code is apologizing and doing what your parents ask."

This means that if your child wants to watch a favorite show, go to a friend's house, go to a game or practice, or do anything other than sit around and read, the child will first need to do what you asked. If the child starts to get upset about being grounded, you'll need to correct this perception. They are not being grounded. The child can go to a friend's, go to the game, and so on, as soon as the child does what you ask. The child's life is on hold. He or she is in control of the situation. The longer the child delays, the longer he or she has to wait to play.

Your child also will need to be aware that the more effort you have to exert to get him or her to do what you requested, the more effort the child will have to make to get to play. If you have to spend 30 minutes trying to calm your child down and convincing the child to do what you've asked, the child will need to do something to give you back a bit of your energy (this could be doing a small chore; writing you a nice note; making an "I'm sorry" card for you; playing a song you like on the piano or guitar; or preparing a snack for you), as well as do what you originally asked. The idea is that if you drain someone of energy, you need to do something to pay them back. If the child yells at you, calls you names, or uses vulgar language, the child will need to learn other strategies for expressing frustration. However, I'll talk about that in the next lesson.

One of the things I like about this approach is that the child is never "backed into a corner." Kids with ADHD tend to get aggressive when they are told that they have messed up and there is nothing they can do to get what they want. During the period of agitation, they can say and do some very hurtful things. If the parents somehow stick to their guns and persist in denying their child what is wanted because the child "didn't earn it" or "misbehaved," they are often in for a couple of hours of misery. At the end of it, the parent will often end up doing something to cheer up the child, which in essence negates the effect of the punishment.

With Time Stands Still, children effectively determine how long they will be denied the opportunity to do what they wanted to do. Their actions also will determine the kinds of actions needed to make up. I've learned that kids with ADHD have an incredibly well-developed sense of fairness. It is not hard to teach the idea that they control the duration of their punishment, or that they will need to make up for hurtful actions. They know what it feels like to be hurt. They also learn pretty quickly that they have no one to blame but themselves if they are delayed in doing something that they like.

HOMEWORK

At this point, I want you to decide which teaching strategy you'd like to begin using. I discussed Charting approaches and Work for Play Plans, plus Time Stands Still. All can be useful, and your choice depends on your style. If you are a person who prefers written contracts and are fairly well organized,

Charting may work. If you have difficulties remembering details and tend to be disorganized, the Work for Play Plan and Time Stands Still methods may work better for you. Decide on one.

Next, select your goals from the "Top 40" list. As I said at the beginning of this lesson, keep it simple. Start with a few goals (six or so) and expand from there. Usually parents will select a group of goals to begin with and link privileges and rewards to those behaviors. You can use a point system or you can divide the day into parts, tell the child what is needed to "earn free time" for each time period, and take it from there. However, with either approach it is important to remember that "outrageous" behaviors (yelling, hitting, defying) must always be part of the program. In other words, it's fine if you want to reward your child for doing chores or homework, but if the child calls you a name, or hits you, then the child will need to perform some type of corrective behavior (Time Stands Still).

After you decide on the type of parenting strategy and select your initial goals, sit down and do several dry runs with another adult. Review what your child needs to do to earn privileges. Make sure it makes sense to you before you tell your child. When you inform your child, let the child know that your decision was made because he or she is no longer a "little kid." Your child needs to hear some version of the following:

> When you were a baby, you might get what you wanted by crying, yelling, and pounding. That was because

there wasn't any other way for you to let us know what you needed. Now you're a lot older and one of my jobs as your parent is to teach you other ways to get what you want in life. Since part of growing up is learning that you need to earn what you want, we're going to start doing that in our home. Here's how it will work.

This lesson is not to be limited to your child with ADHD. If you are developing a plan for your child with ADHD, you should decide on one for your other children as well. Their program may include different lessons because they don't have ADHD. However, because most of us need to learn something, I am certain you will be able to decide on lessons that you'd like each of your children to learn.

8

Temperament May Be Inherited ... but ... Emotional Control Is Learned

Now that you selected the lessons you want your child to learn, an obvious question is staring you in the face. What do you do when your child has a huge tantrum because he or she doesn't like your "lesson plan"? Let's be honest. Most kids are not going to thank you for teaching them how to organize their rooms, complete their homework, get to bed on time, or eat a healthy variety of foods. There will be times when your child rages about the unfairness of life or broods about how he or she "never gets to do anything" and how she "wishes I were dead" or "someone else was my parent." Although some kids will have lots of emotional meltdowns, others will take frustration in stride. A child's temperament is one reason for these differences in emotional reactivity. The other primary reason centers on the lessons you teach your child about how to develop emotional control, overcome frustration, and solve problems that come up in life.

If you are the parent of more than one child, you probably have noticed differences in the temperament of your children, almost from birth. Some babies display the serenity of Gandhi, calmly and peacefully surveying the world. They lie in their cribs and occupy themselves looking at their mobiles while slurping on their fingers and toes. Nothing seems to trouble these kids. They easily accept smoochies from grandma, grandpa, and anyone else in the family.

On the other hand, there are kids who seem uninterested in faces and physical contact with family and friends. Occasionally, such children will have strong reactions to hugs, often yelling, screaming, and arching away. These children may seem "independent," "strong-willed," or "high strung," showing anger over minor frustrations.

As babies grow, such differences in temperament continue. Some are highly active and quite loud, climbing on and over any object (including you) and screaming while they do so. They may take apart anything that isn't sealed tightly and work intensely to open anything that is. Any change in their daily schedule or frustration of their demands is met by a wall of tears or by rage. At the other extreme, there are kids who are content to occupy themselves quietly while looking at picture books, watching television, or playing with toys. When it's time to stop play and go with mom or dad, it's no big deal. As parents, you have, I hope, fully realized that your parenting style did not cause these traits.

If you happen to be the parent of one child, you may also have noticed the differences between your child's "temperament" and that of other children. I hope you have recognized that you did not cause these differences. The use of the term "temperament" typically refers to traits such as the activity level of the child, the degree of inquisitiveness, and the way a child interacts with others and handles frustration. Is the child engaging or withdrawn? Shy or outgoing? Calm or easily upset? Cheerful and optimistic or moody and complaining? Although there is considerable variability in the energy level and emotional reactivity of all of us, one reality cannot be avoided. That is that we all need to learn acceptable ways to express needs, tolerate temporary delays in satisfying our desires, solve interpersonal problems, and control our emotional reactions when we are disappointed or frightened. As with the other lessons discussed, you will be your child's primary teacher, this time in the area of emotional and behavioral control.

In this lesson, I discuss strategies to help your child develop emotional control and inhibit impulsive behaviors (such as interrupting, intruding, and demanding that needs be met immediately). Children, teens, and adults with ADHD commonly struggle with at least one of the following three types of emotional problems: outbursts of anger; excessive worry; and depressive reactions. The intensity of these reactions is far, far, greater than would be expected for the child's age group, often leading parents, teachers, and counselors to wonder if a child is really depressed or a victim of abuse. The following is an example.

Recently I received a phone call from a highly concerned school social worker. One of my patients had become massively upset when he received his teacher "rating" for that afternoon. Apparently, he had not wanted to work on a particular school task and resisted for a while. Although his teacher was able to coax him into working, he did not receive a smiley-face sticker for that time period. No big deal . . . right?

Well, when he saw the "face" without the smile, he freaked. He pounded his fist on his desk and pushed his papers and pencils off the desk, striking other students. He then proceeded to pound his head on the desk saying, "I'm an idiot, I'm an idiot" . . . followed by, "I'm going home and kill myself." He refused to do any more school work and after much thrashing about, was led to the social worker's office.

Once he got to the social worker's office, he continued to talk about wanting to kill himself. Like any trained professional, the social worker evaluated the risk for suicide. Did he have a plan? Yep, he was going to go home, climb onto the roof of his house, and jump off. Was his mother going to be home so she could stop this? Nope, she was at work; only his older sister (a teenager) would be there. Clearly alarmed, the social worker contacted the mother and me. The social worker wondered if she needed to take the patient to the emergency room of the hospital for crisis intervention. So far, this chain of events would make a lot of sense. Except for one detail. The child has ADHD.

What Does ADHD Have to Do With a Suicide Threat?

Long ago, when I first started treating kids diagnosed with ADHD, I might have done the same thing the social worker did. After all, there is a student in your office threatening suicide and the child has a plan that could certainly cause harm. That was before I realized that my patients would often have incredibly intense reactions to situations that didn't seem to merit it, such as threatening to kill themselves or run away because their parents wouldn't buy them a toy or take them somewhere. They would call themselves "stupid" or "an idiot," or say "I wish I were dead" because they couldn't figure out a math problem.

What I learned over the years is that most often, the causes of my patients' intense emotional reactions had more to do with the neurology of ADHD and adequacy of their diet, sleeping patterns, medication, educational plan, and communication and problem-solving abilities than with any type of trauma. This is very different from what causes such reactions in children and teens who don't have ADHD.

The school example illustrates these differences. What if a child who didn't have ADHD had a melt-down over not getting a smiley face? Let's say this child talked about how he was going to kill himself. With such a child, I'd be very concerned about what was going on. I'd look to figure out what possibly could be triggering such a reaction in a child who typically did not show this type of behavior. Chances are that some pretty upsetting events had occurred or were occurring in that child's life.

On the other hand, if a child with ADHD starts expressing depressing or hostile thoughts because he or she didn't get a smiley-face sticker, my experience is that it is likely that medication needs to be adjusted, diet examined, educational plan reviewed, or the parents' lesson plan for teaching problem-solving and anger control skills needs to be revised. As I discuss in this lesson, most children with ADHD respond well to a combination of medication; instruction in certain self-calming, problem-solving, social skills, and confidence building techniques; and parental reinforcement of appropriate behavior when frustrated.

However, although psychological factors are not at the root of most of the emotional or behavioral outbursts displayed by children with ADHD, it is important to realize that there are some children with ADHD who have experienced trauma, abuse, or neglect, and that these children require psychological treatment. At my clinic, when a child continues to display intense anger, chronic depression, or debilitating anxiety despite a sustained period (6 months) of pharmacological, nutritional, educational, and parental intervention, exploration of potential trauma, abuse, or neglect is often quite helpful.

With this in mind, let's think about what has happened when you have tried to help your child with ADHD "calm down" or "cheer up" when he or she has gotten upset. I am certain you have attempted to have a rational conversation with an ADHD child when the child was angry, frightened, or sad. What was that like? Were you able to discover the root of the intense emotional reaction and sanely address it? Highly unlikely! Remember that earlier in this book I talked about the role of the frontal lobe of the brain. Well, the frontal lobe has several "jobs." One has to do with "focused attention." However, another important role involves helping us "think through" situations that frustrate us and decide on an effective plan of action.

Most kids with ADHD have frontal lobes that are not sufficiently active. As a result, when they need to pay attention or concentrate on school work, it is harder for them to do so. Similarly, when they are disappointed, frustrated, or scared, it is harder for them to use the "thinking" part of their brain to help control their emotional reactions and figure out another way to handle the situation. Until the rage or terror reaction subsides a bit, there is really no rational "talking" about the situation. Even more puzzling is the dramatic change that occurs in a child with ADHD within 10 minutes of the event, if the parent, teacher, or counselor can stop "feeding" the emotional fire.

How Can I Not "Feed" My Kid's Emotional Fire?

Let's go back to the story of my "suicidal" patient. When I spoke to the school social worker, I asked if she was aware of what my patient would lose because of the teacher's rating. The social worker told me that the patient and his mother had made a "deal" for that day. The plan was this: If the child was able to get a smiley face for his effort and behavior for all four quarters of the day (we had divided the school day into four parts), he could go to his basketball game that night.

I encouraged the counselor to tell my patient that I would speak with his mother about their deal and see if there was a way that he could "make up" for his mistake. However, the child needed to calm down (take some deep breaths, sip a little water or juice), regroup, and cooperate with his teacher for the rest of the day. The counselor was asked to remind my patient that, as with other times when the child had been disappointed and upset, he and his mom would figure out what to do to take care of the problem. The counselor also contacted his mother to make sure that an adult could be home after school.

When I spoke with the patient's mother, we reviewed several issues. One had to do with the "all or nothing" type of deal. These are real setups for meltdowns. Kids with ADHD are unlikely to be "perfect," so linking any type of reward for being perfect is unlikely to work. One goal behind reinforcement programs is to encourage effort, and my patient was certainly motivated to earn his reward. However, a secondary goal of any reinforcement program is to help a child learn how to control emotional reactions to frustration or disappointment. My patient was not so successful on that end, so my discussion with the mother centered on these two goals.

First, we looked at her child's effort for the day. Generally, it was quite good. After all, three smiley faces out of four is "not too shabby" (to quote Adam Sandler). But the child did "poop out" at the end and tried to avoid school work. . .not a good idea. We had to address that. In addition, his reaction to disappointment needed to improve. Here's what made sense to us. Because the child had resisted doing work at school, he needed to complete that assignment at home, plus some extra work, before mom would even consider letting him go to his game. Second, because he had done things that had frightened other people (kids in his class, his teacher, and the school social worker), he needed to do something to help them feel a little more relaxed.

At this point, my patient had to make a decision. He could refuse to do the work and not go to the game, or he could accept responsibility, perform corrective action, and make amends. He chose to do the schoolwork (plus an extra assignment), and he decided to make a card for his teacher and for the social worker that included a joke from *Reader's Digest* (he cut it out) and some simple words to let them know he was sorry for worrying them, but he was okay and was working on handling his anger better. He wasn't able to go out after school (because he was working on these tasks), but his mom let him go to the game because he took responsibility for his actions, performed a corrective action (i.e., doing the "avoided work" plus an extra task), and took action to demonstrate sensitivity to the feelings of others.

The key elements in our plan were to continue to encourage the child's effort and emotional control, and to help him realize that there are consequences when he tries to avoid work and when he loses his "control." As I say throughout this book, it is important for parents to be clear about their lesson plan. Certainly, his mother could have stuck to her guns and held her line: "No four smiley faces . . . no basketball for you!" However, she is likely to have spent the rest of the day dealing with a determined, angry child who would pester her until it was too late to go to the game.

Of course, this mom could have kept piling on even more punishments for the child's behavior, which in turn would trigger another burst of emotional fire. I've seen kids with ADHD lose all privileges for a week within a few minutes because of their reaction to disappointment. However, at the end of the day, one of these kids is not likely to say: "I was wrong to give my teacher and parents a hard time. I know I need to do my work and try harder tomorrow." Nope. If mom had held her hard line, adding punishments to the predictable outburst of begging, whining, tears, and rage, her son would have ended the night saying some version of, "my mom's a jerk . . . I hate her." If the child had lost privileges for the rest of the week, there would be less motivation for him to try tomorrow. This can lead to a real downward spiral because a lack of effort at school will lead to fewer "smiley" faces, further punishment, etc., etc., etc.

TOOLS FOR EXTINGUISHING EMOTIONAL FIRES AND TEACHING CONTROL

Think about a time when your child had a meltdown. Ask yourself, "What did I want to teach?" "What was my lesson plan?" "How did my plan work?" As you are trying to reconstruct the scene, consider these keys for extinguishing emotional fires.

Key 1: Help the Child Find a Safe Place to Cool Off

What do you do when you're angry? Do you go and start talking to the person who "ticked" you off, or to a passerby? As you have discovered, that is probably not a good idea. The reason? Anger is an emotional state intended to prepare us for a fight or to intimidate another person. During the time we are angry, the regions of the brain that are needed to solve a problem are not activated. They are suppressed. Consequently, the last thing that we should do when angry is talk to another person.

Step one in learning how to control anger is to remember not to speak to another person during that time . . . it will only lead to more trouble. Instead, your child needs to learn some ways to get the feeling to subside a bit. Here are some ideas.

At School

A child can be given permission to see the school counselor, psychologist, nurse, or to take a walk with an aide. Children with ADHD who have a problem with anger control at school need to have such a plan in their IEP. That way, the teacher does not have to figure out what to say or do with a child who is obviously agitated, and the child would know that there is a way out of the situation without getting into further trouble. At the counselor's office, the child could work with clay or paint, listen to some music, sit in a comfy chair and grip a koosh ball (or stress ball), or take out a piece of paper and write (or type) everything the child wanted to say (but didn't). The children are encouraged to use some type of physical release to get the body to calm down a bit. Teaching kids the benefits of deep, slow breathing is my favorite stress releasing activity.

Another strategy I like to use is the "Emotional Garbage Bag" technique. Here's how it works. The Emotional Garbage Bag technique requires a paper bag, a piece of paper rolled into a megaphone, or some object that the child can "yell into." The counselor can let the child know that when a person gets angry, there is a lot of "garbage" that builds up inside us and that we need to get rid of it before we can figure out what to do. The child is encouraged to take the bag, put it over his or her mouth and say anything. If the child wants a target, the counselor can challenge the child to see if she or he can blow the bottom out of the bag with the force of their words. The bottom line is this: Before we try to figure out what to do, the child needs to reduce his or her anger. I tell my patients that it is not a good idea to talk to others when angry . . . so I practice what I preach in my sessions with them.

At Home

Cooling off by doing any non-destructive physical activity is a good idea (lifting weights, riding a stationary bike, hopping on a treadmill, playing an instrument, doing yoga exercises, doing push-ups or sit-ups). Listening to music, playing with clay or blocks, or using the Emotional Garbage Bag technique also can help. Because physically aggressive and destructive behaviors (pounding pillows, hitting a punching bag, kicking a ball) can establish a dangerous pattern for adult years, I do not encourage teaching children that engaging in aggressive behavior leads to a sense of physical release. I also find it useful for parents to teach their kids that re-establishing deep, slow breathing is a highly effective way to calm anger, particularly if the child breathes and remains quiet until the child can answer two questions: "What do you want? . . . What can you do to make it happen?" After the child is calm and has the answer to these two questions, effective problem solving can begin.

Again, the key point to stress in your teaching is that we can talk about what to do when the child's anger subsides. I encourage parents to remind the child that you will be glad to talk with her or him once the child has calmed down, but that you don't talk to people who are angry. If the child refuses to leave and insists on yelling at you, quietly remind him or her that the longer the yelling and screaming continues, the more the child will need to do to make up for this decision. At that point, don't struggle with the child or try to force the child anywhere. However, when the child is finished, he or she will need to apologize to you (for not obeying you) and do whatever corrective action you consider appropriate.

Key 2: Identify the Child's Needs and Help Develop a Plan

When a child with ADHD is having an emotional outburst, identifying the child's need and developing a viable solution is crucial. As a parent or counselor, it may feel as though you are walking into a sea of emotional waves, but I encourage you to keep trying to bring the child to "shore" by encouraging her or him to remain quiet and continue breathing until the child can identify the need and a way to "make it happen." What did the child want or not want? Was it something that another child said or did? (*What did the child want?*) Was it a comment from a teacher? (*What did the child want?*) Was it a request to do work that the child does not know how to do? (*What did the child want?*) Was it the child's fear of your emotional reaction after school? In each case, the questions remain the same ... "What did the child want? ... What can they do to make it happen?" I tell my patients, "When you can answer these questions, your brain is back in the game. Until you can answer these questions, the only thing that can come from talking is more trouble."

Key 3: Help the Child Realize That if He "Blew Up" at Another Person, He Will Need to Apologize and Make "Amends" Before You Will Consider the Source of His Frustration

After clarifying the nature of the need, you and your child can work on the problem at hand. As you do so, it is critical to realize that you are trying to help a child learn how to control emotional reactions and solve problems. If the child has yelled at or threatened another person, she or he will need to apologize and do something to "make up." This doesn't have to be huge, but something needs to be done to reinforce the notion that if you "mess up" you need to "make up."

Key 4: Help the Child Learn Alternative Ways to Achieve a Personal Goal

Much as I hate to quote the Rolling Stones, a line from one of their songs has always made a lot of sense to me. I use it a lot (which must date me). The lyric is this: "You can't always get what you want, but if you try, sometimes, you get what you need." In life, we don't always get what we want. But if we can fight the urge to rage or despair and get our "frontal lobes" into the game, typically we can figure out a way to get what we want or something just as satisfying. Let's play this out in a real life situation.

A common problem that occurs at my office centers on where the family will eat dinner after their appointment with me. I have always preferred to locate my clinic on a street that has a variety of choices. In fact, I can easily boast that there is probably no clinic on the East Coast that has as many fast food choices within one mile as mine. Name a food chain. Burger King? Got one. McDonald's? Got two (try to beat that). Wendy's? Yep. Arby's? Yep. KFC? Yep. Subway? Yep. Want Pizza? There's a Pizza Hut, Domino's, Papa John's and some local favorites (like Tony's, Nirchi's, and OIP's) that make my taste buds sing. Need ice cream with that dinner? I've got Friendly's. Give up yet?

Well, with all those choices, it's easy to generate frustration. Say you're thinking Pizza Hut but your child wants McDonald's. On your way to Dr. Monastra's office you make the mistake of bringing up the topic with your child. An argument ensues. The child wants his burger, you want pizza. The kid begs, pleads, whines, sulks, and kicks the front seat. You hold on: "Pizza Hut or nothing," you say. The kid sulks and says, "I hate going to the doctor's and I'm not going in." You say, "If you don't go in, I'm going to _____" (the blank is provided for you to fill in your typical punishment or threat). The kid comes into the office obviously sulking.

After years as a doctor, I've learned that if I react with a quiet, somber approach, the session will get off to a pretty lousy start. So I'd probably give the kid a great big greeting, toss a koosh ball in his direction, or see if he'll give me a hand on a "Lego" design I was working on upstairs. I'd try any type of diversion that I could think of to get him moving (e.g., "Could you help me get a drink?" or "Could you help me figure out where I left the afternoon snacks that I keep around for my patients?").

Once upstairs (and away from the waiting room audience), I'd mention in passing that it looked as though he was disappointed about something. Then I'd hear about the dinner tragedy. I'd check out how bad it had gotten in the car (did he say anything horrific to his mom or dad). I'd do that because I try to teach my patients that no matter how right you are, you need to apologize and make up for mean things that you say or do. If the child wanted to discuss this further, we'd go over ways to approach the parents. For example, when the child saw the parents, the child could apologize and ask if there was anything she or he needed to do to make up for the actions that took place in the car. Then the child could ask if there was anything that could be done to convince them to go to McDonald's. If there was really nothing that could be done this time, then the child could try to obtain something else or discuss a way to get an agreement to eat at McDonald's the next time. The key element is to try to help the child learn how to solve problems by collaborating with (rather than bullying) others. I focus on this in the next lesson, and you'll get to play the role of parent–counselor.

Meltdowns in Other Public Places

This brings me to another common "meltdown" arena, the mall (or other outside shopping or recreational sites). Most parents try to prepare in advance for trips to these types of places. They are high-risk places for begging, whining, full-blown tantrums (when the child doesn't get his or her way), and general misery for parents. As a result, parents are advised to go over the ground rules with their children long before they leave the house and again before they get out of the car. If the child is going to be able to buy something, be clear about how much money he or she can spend and when it can be spent. If the child is not going to be able to buy anything but can earn a trip to a fast food restaurant, spell out what the child needs to do. It is important that you don't back yourself into a corner on this one. Here's an example of what I mean.

Let's say you're headed to the mall. You tell your children that you are going to get them sneakers. If they stay close to you, don't whine, and don't beg, then they can get a meal at Burger King. Sounds good, right? Hardly. From the minute you hit the mall, your child with ADHD is distracted by the wonder of it all and is begging to go into Video Game World, the arcade, the toy store, or any other place that seems neat. You say, "No," again, and again, and again. Finally, you blow up and tell your child, "No Burger King." The child goes ballistic. Big scene in the mall. All eyes are on you. You feel like an idiot. You are furious with your child and you exit the mall without sneakers. Don't feel bad if this has happened to you. It has happened to most (if not all) of us.

Think back on some of the earlier lessons. Remember the basic principle: if you want a child to learn, there needs to be a clear instruction given and a well-defined reason to learn. In addition, I talked about how the opportunity to earn what a child wants tends to promote improved effort. On the other hand, parental punishment and removal of privileges really activates aggressive reactions in kids with ADHD. This is not to say that kids with ADHD should always get what they want. It just means that these kids will learn much more from earning or failing to earn (their responsibility) rather than parental punishment or withdrawal of privileges (translates to "the parents' fault").

In the situation I just described, what is the instruction? "Stay close, don't whine, and don't beg." Okay, that seems clear. Well, maybe not. How many times can the child wander, whine, or beg before the deal is off? Is it the first whine or the thirtieth? The first beg or the fiftieth? What it usually boils down to is how many times can the child not do what he or she was supposed to do before you blow up? You might think that it is highly understandable that the child loses Burger King after the tenth whine. But how did number ten differ from number nine? Who was to know that the deal was nine and out?

Here are a couple of ideas that may be useful. Let's say you are using a point system or "chart" at home. You could say that for every 5 or 10 minutes (depending on age) that the child stays with you, doesn't beg, and doesn't whine, the child earns a point. If it helps, they could even hold the watch or timer and keep track for you. The child needs a certain number of points to get to Burger King but if the child doesn't earn BK, then the child can use the points when you get home. However, as with other types of misbehavior, you will need to decide if the child needs to make amends when you get home.

If you aren't using a point system, you could still use the 5- or 10-minute time approach and tell the child that he or she earns a quarter (or whatever seems reasonable) to use at Burger King (or another store) for each period that the rules are followed. For every period, you can hand the child a penny or some type of token that can be exchanged for quarters at the desired location. If the child hasn't earned enough to buy a meal, then you will save it for the next trip to the mall. Again, if the child has a meltdown, it is pointless to try to "reason" with the child. It's probably best to leave the mall, regroup in the car (if possible), or try another time.

Remember, regardless of the intensity of your child's reaction, you are still the teacher. The child can yell and scream all she or he wants. If you have been requiring that the child apologize and make up for misbehavior, your child (at some level) realizes that she or he will need to apologize eventually and make "amends" for disobeying and giving you a hard time, as discussed in Time Stands Still. You don't have to make a public showing of your power. You are trying to teach your child emotional control. Your loss of control won't teach that. Repeating the process in which your child apologizes and "makes it right" with you will help the child learn. You don't have to win "the battle of the mall" in front of bystanders. A calm reminder that the more the child misbehaves, the more he or she will need to do to make up is usually sufficient to get everyone moving out of the mall.

What About Medication to Help With Anger Control Problems?

There is a lot of debate about the use of medications in treating "emotional" problems in children. In some respects it parallels a broader issue among adults. After all, shouldn't people be able to control anger without resorting to "drugs"? Doesn't this communicate that street drugs are "okay"? Won't it all lead to increased drug abuse among kids with ADHD? And finally, doesn't it mean that you are some type of defective parent if you even consider such a treatment?

A person's answers to these questions reveals his or her level of knowledge when it comes to the kinds of emotional problems that people with different types of medical conditions can develop. Let's take diabetes, for example. If a person has a body that produces an insufficient amount of insulin, that person will have difficulty processing "sugars." This condition is called diabetes. The American public is generally quite aware of this condition and considers it to be a "legitimate" medical condition. In fact, if a parent, grandparent, aunt, or uncle with diabetes started to seem extra tired, confused, grumpy, or outright hostile, family and friends might ask if the person has eaten that day or checked blood sugar levels. With diabetic patients, the use of medication (and proper diet) serves several important roles. It helps stabilize blood sugar levels, which in turn improves attention, concentration, energy level, and mood. This doesn't mean that people with diabetes don't need to learn ways to control mood and solve personal problems. It just means that we need to attend to their medical care as part of the treatment.

Now let's consider a person with the medical condition called ADHD. Scientific evidence to date indicates that this condition is related to brain function, particularly in the level of activity in brain regions that are responsible for attention, concentration, mood regulation, and behavioral control. The most commonly prescribed medications primarily target those regions involved in attention and behavioral control. These are stimulant medications like Ritalin, Adderall, Metadate, Concerta, and Dexedrine. When administered in a carefully titrated dose and in a context of adequate nutrition, these medications can help a child succeed in learning a number of skills, including the lessons described for controlling anger.

However, there are times when stimulant medications do not provide sufficient improvement in regions of the brain responsible for anger control. In those instances, several other types of medications may prove helpful. One type of treatment involves antidepressant medications (like Zoloft). Zoloft promotes the activity of "calming" neural pathways that use the brain chemical serotonin. These neural networks are the ones that help to control agitation and anger. When taken in combination with a stimulant medication, this type of medication can help patients improve attention, impulse control, and mood regulation.

Another treatment consists of antihypertensive medications (like Catapres). These are the medications that individuals with high blood pressure take so that everyday stresses and frustrations do not significantly elevate blood pressure. They work by occupying brain receptors that are sensitive to adrenalin, a hormone that is released when we are experiencing frustrating or dangerous situations. When a patient with ADHD uses this type of medication, the patient is less likely to have aggressive outbursts over minimal frustrations. This type of medication can be used in combination with stimulants; however, monitoring of blood pressure is needed to prevent excessive sedation.

Depression, Phobias, and Other Anxiety Reactions

Up to this point, I spent a lot of time discussing ways to help a child address feelings of anger and frustration. However, children with ADHD struggle with other types of emotional reactions, too. Among the most alarming are the expressions of depression and the near paralyzing levels of anxiety that can occur. I've watched kids burst out in tears, telling parents that they hated their lives and were going to commit suicide because they were being grounded for failing a course. I've heard stories about and have seen kids with ADHD who were nearly mute. These kids would go through extended periods of time in which they seem quite somber and unenthused about life, and spend their time just lounging around watching television for hours on end.

Certainly, the lack of emotional control during times of disappointment or frustration is not a unique trait of children and teens with ADHD. Let's face it, we all need to learn how to shake off the blues sometimes. However, certain kids with ADHD just don't seem thrilled about any part of life, whereas others react as if the slightest disappointment is the end of the world. To help kids with ADHD develop a bit more resilience to deal with "disappointment" and reduce the degree of "depression," several strategies seem to help. I describe each in detail.

The first suggestion I give to my "depressed" kids with ADHD (and their parents) involves increasing the number of "enjoyable" activities that they do each day. Similar to eating "three squares a day," I encourage them to make sure that every day they do three things they like. These little presents don't have to be huge. Just simple stuff. Could be making sure that they get to watch a particular television show that they like. Could be getting the chance to snuggle and read a book with mom or dad. Could be a family game of Yahtzee. Could be wearing a favorite sweater to school. Could be getting together with a friend. Could be listening to a CD. Could be making sure that they always have something they like for lunch (one of my favorites). Bottom line: Doing three pleasurable activities each day is a good "antidepressant" for anyone.

Another antidepressant strategy involves daily physical activity. Research evidence suggests that individuals can reduce symptoms of depression by engaging in activities such as walking, swimming, jogging, or biking. I include research references on this topic in this book's list of supplemental readings, in case you're interested. For kids, this translates to playing sports like baseball, soccer, football, swimming, wrestling, lacrosse, basketball; practicing karate, gymnastics, or dance; playing hide-and-seek, man-hunt, or any other activity that involves getting the body in motion. Parents are advised to ensure that one of the "requirements" of daily life is that their child engages in such activities.

A third strategy ties into the concept of self-esteem. People who are depressed often do not feel very good about themselves. Here are some self-esteem boosters to consider. First, it is important that a person feel that he or she "looks good" in the eyes of the parents. It is important that your child hear you say you love her or him, and it is helpful for you to point out the times when you actually are proud of them. Another booster shot involves helping your child "get good" at something that other kids of the same age respect or admire. Although it may be wonderful that your child develops awesome skills at the piano, this is not likely to help with self-esteem until late adolescence or college age. If your child loves playing the piano, riding horses, painting, and the like, great. However, try to make sure that the child is helped to get good at the kinds of activities that other kids in the neighborhood are involved in (roller blading, surfing, sports, fishing, skiing, learning an instrument and forming a band with friends, or joining a gymnastics, dance, or karate club).

Another self-esteem boost comes from having at least one friend in the class. If your child routinely gets together with other kids in his or her class, great. If not, try to do what you can to learn the phone numbers of other kids in the class and try to find ways to invite classmates over for informal gatherings or trips to a nearby park, fishing hole, lake, etc. Help your child find out what clubs, teams, or activities their classmates are in, and pave the way for your child to join up. For kids who live a distance from classmates, connecting with kids at church groups, the YMCA or YWCA, a Boys' & Girls' Club, or interest groups (like gymnastics, swimming, karate, or microd-racing clubs) can be helpful. Although you may need to add "participating in an activity with classmates" to the list of your child's daily responsibilities, it will be well worth it.

Finally, we all feel better if we have a sense that we have some degree of control over our lives. Although you are the boss of the family, your child would get a boost if he or she has the sense that he or she has control over certain things. Could be clothes. Could be the color of the bedroom walls. Could be the choice of meal on one day per week. Could be the choice of one family activity per month. It's your call. Have some fun with this.

My Child is Too Terrified to Do Anything With Other Kids. What Can I Do?

Anxiety and phobic reactions are common among my patients. Again, medications can be a very important part of treatment. Some of my patients respond well to antidepressant medications like Paxil. Paxil is a medication that works by enhancing the "calming" effect of neural pathways that use the brain chemical serotonin. Like Zoloft, Paxil is considered an SSRI-type antidepressant; however, it seems to work more like an anti-anxiety medicine and can be combined with stimulants to help with attention and anxiety. However, as with any medication, side effects (depression) have been reported with Paxil, so I encourage you to consider other strategies before using an SSRI for anxiety.

Another type of medical approach involves the use of antihypertensive medications, such as Tenex. Similar to Catapres, Tenex works by occupying brain receptors sensitive to adrenalin. Tenex is a medication that seems particularly useful in calming obsessive–compulsive symptoms and severe anxiety reactions. It, too, can be combined with stimulants; however, careful monitoring of blood pressure and cardiac functioning is required.

Isn't There Something I Can Do Besides Give My Child Medication?

In addition to medications, there are several strategies that can be used by parents to reduce fears. Each of these strategies is founded on the following well-established principle: "If we face what we fear and experience a sense of calmness (or a relaxed state) while we are in the fear-evoking situation, then our fears begin to subside." I start with a simple example and expand from there.

I knew a child who was afraid to go outside because she had been told (by a friend) that if she touched a particular type of bug, she would turn into that bug. So, what can you as a parent do? Well, most of us would start off by trying to convince the child that there was nothing to worry about. That approach will often go nowhere fast. I learned a long time ago that you cannot reason away fears. It eventually boils down to a person's decision to enter into the "fear" zone and take a chance that he or she will survive. Now the word of an expert (like a parent) might help, but the odds are high that some type of direct exposure will be needed. So, we talked about the truth (touching a snail will not turn you into a slug) and went outside and just looked at some for a while. However, the turning point came when I showed the child that touching was safe (by touching one), and we both saw that I survived.

This example of the bug phobia is just one example of the kinds of fears kids have. Some are afraid to go alone into parts of the house or apartment. In those cases, I often encourage parents to play a kind of "hide and seek" game in which the parent hides boxes in different parts of the house. Some will contain little gifts (e.g., a snack, a dime, or a ticket for game time with dad or mom). Other boxes will contain words of encouragement (e.g., "I can't believe you were brave enough to go under the bed . . . I'm proud of you."). Still others might contain something that the child is afraid of (e.g., a jar with a spider in it). As the child searches for little prizes, the child overcomes the fears.

Another common fear involves sleeping alone at night. Although it may seem easier to just give in to our child's desire, once children get into the habit of sleeping with their parents they strenuously resist sleeping alone. In addition to the obvious restriction on parental intimacy, when a child is allowed to sleep with mom and dad it contributes to avoidance of facing one of the earliest fears that must be mastered: "I can be okay even when I am not in my parents' presence." Because confidence comes from facing fears, your permission to allow a child to sleep with you prevents the child from developing the self-esteem that comes from overcoming this fear.

When kids have a fear of sleeping alone, I often use the following approach. We start out by establishing a specific time for going to the child's bedroom each night. In addition, we make sure that the child does not snack on high-energy foods (e.g., cookies, cereal, and so on, before bedtime). Until the child is consistently sleeping alone, I want to make sure the child is not on a sugar high as he or she is trying to go to sleep.

The next step involves moving a chair for the parent into the child's room. This chair needs to be comfortable enough so the parent could sit a while and read the paper or a book (with the assistance of one of those miniature book lights), as the child falls asleep. With the lights on in the room, the parent can read to the child, either while sitting on the edge of the child's bed or in the parent chair. However, after reading, the lights need to be dimmed and the child is to stay in bed. The parent informs the child that she or he will stay in the room and watch over the child until the child falls asleep. There is minimal conversation after this point. As with any skill, it is often helpful for the parent to give the child a reason for learning to face this fear. It could be the opportunity to do some activity the next day, the opportunity to earn money toward a prize at the end of the week, or being able to have a favorite breakfast or lunch item the next day. Letting the child know that he or she will "feel so proud when (he or she) can sleep alone" in the bed also can help.

After the child demonstrates that she or he can fall asleep within 15 minutes with the parent in the room, the parent chair is moved to the doorway. The process remains the same. There is a reading time with the child and then "quiet time." The parent remains in the doorway in the chair until the child demonstrates that she or he can fall asleep within 15 minutes on a consistent basis. At this point, the parent can then begin to go outside of the child's room after reading. The parent typically will need to be on the same floor of the house until the child falls asleep.

Now as with any plan, there can be problems with this one. Your child may refuse to stay in bed and may insist on sitting on your lap. As with any refusal, I encourage you to let the child know that the longer the child resists and the more work the child causes for you, the more work the child will need to do for you the next day before he or she can play. Another typical problem occurs if the child wakes up in the middle of the night and calls out for you. Much as you'd rather stay in bed, I encourage you to tuck your child in and remain in your "parent chair" until the child falls asleep.

Even though this may seem like a lot of work, facing the fear of the dark at bedtime contributes to a child's sense of power and confidence. Although there are children's books and videos that can help a bit, in the end it will boil down to your child's decision to face these fears. It is essential for the development of confidence that your child (and you) succeed at this task.

For kids who generally seem anxious, I also use a kind of bravery game. Again, awarding points, privileges, or activities for facing fears is recommended. In the bravery game, parents work with their child to develop a list of activities and things that the child fears. After the list is developed, parents can teach their child about the calming effect of controlled breathing, and the parents can then help their child to face one fear per day or week. When I teach a child (or anyone) about controlling anxiety by controlling breathing, the person is initially quite doubtful until I demonstrate. Here's a lesson that you might find useful.

I begin the lesson by telling kids one important truth: "You can't feel anxiety if your body has plenty of oxygen (air)." I continue with some version of, "When we are in a situation that scares us a bit, the first thing that happens is that we stop breathing. We freeze. As soon as we stop breathing, our heart goes into overdrive. It starts beating faster and faster, trying to get the little bit of oxygen to all the body parts that it can. We feel that as 'anxiety' or 'fear' or 'worry'. The more worry we feel, the less we breathe. This keeps our heart going faster and faster and faster until we feel dizzy and might even pass out. We try to tell ourselves to calm down, but it doesn't work. Usually, the worry only fades when we run away (or avoid) the situation. That works fine for the time being, but it doesn't help us get over our fears."

"So, if you want to get over your fear, the most important thing you need to learn is to feed your body some oxygen (or air) as soon as you start to worry. As soon as you start giving your body some nice, deep, nose-fills of air, you're on the way to feeling great again. Once your body starts to get some air, your heart doesn't have to work so hard. It can start to slow down. As you feel your heart slow down, you'll feel less worried, and pretty soon, you're okay. You just need to remember that the heart might need you to give it at least 15 to 20 slow, deep nose-fills before it has enough air for your body." I practice this a bit with the child. Try this with your kid (or yourself). You'll be amazed.

HOMEWORK

In this lesson, I review ways to help your child with such common emotional problems as outbursts of anger, depressed mood, fears, and anxiety. If your child is struggling with any of these problems, now is a good time for you to sit back and think about your plan to teach the child ways to control these emotional states. You may decide to contact your doctor and try medication as part of the plan. That is absolutely fine. There is no extra credit given for parenting without medicine. My hope is that you will decide on a "lesson plan" to begin to develop your child's confidence, ability to use certain "psychological" strategies to control mood, and satisfaction with daily life. These are among the most important lessons that you will teach your child.

9

Yelling Rarely Solves Anything

I often tell parents that the first lesson they teach their children is that mom and dad will love and care for them. If the child will accept hugs, kisses, and close physical contact during infancy and early childhood, many "I love you's" are smothered on the child without much thought. If the baby smiles, the world opens up to them. If the baby needs a hug, some food, a diaper change, something outside of their grasp, or some play-time, crying will usually get the desired response from a caring parent. However, once a child gets to an age when crying is no longer an "okay" way to get what the child wants (somewhere around age two), problems begin. We not so jokingly refer to this time period as "the terrible twos." After a child learns to speak, crying to get something typically bugs parents. Whining, begging, and throwing tantrums aren't too well appreciated either. Outright defiance of a parent's rules really pushes the buttons.

As we go through the years and our children become teens and young adults, children must learn new

ways to get what they want. At first, they'll use varia-
tions of what worked when they were babies. They'll
cry, whine, yell, and beg. They'll throw tantrums.
They'll regress to the age of three or so and keep asking,
"Why?" "Why do I have to go to bed now?" "Why do
I have to do homework?" "Why can't I buy a new
video game?" "Why do I have to eat breakfast?" Or
they'll beg, "Pleeeeese mommy . . . pleeeese." On and
on and on. Any time you are at the grocery store, or
the local burger place, or the mall, it won't be long
before you see a child much older than three still using
these "baby" strategies to get what the child wants (I
hope it won't be your kid, but hey, it just might be.).
At some point, we come to recognize that there is
another critical lesson that our children need to learn:
*We need to teach children how to "get what you want" while
respecting the needs and concerns of other human beings.*

From the time you and your child awaken, you
are immersed in the process of solving problems. You
need to immediately orchestrate waking, washing,
feeding, and dressing tasks not only for yourself, but
also for your children. Later, you and your children
will need to figure out who is going to cook, clean,
and pick up clothes, toys, and junk. You and the kids
will be involved in negotiating play time, television
time, computer time, homework, chores, bedtime,
meals, etc., etc., etc. You will decide on purchases,
travel to a friend's house, the mall, and so on. These
are just a few of the many decisions that you and your
children will make on a daily basis. How you choose

to handle these decisions determines whether you will end up with a teen who is acting like a "baby" or one who has learned how to solve problems maturely.

TEACHING PROBLEM-SOLVING SKILLS

Let's take a couple of minutes to think about some common ingredients in a typical parent–child argument. Typically, problems occur if there is a conflict of needs or if one person wants something that the other person is afraid to give. If a parent wants a child to do something and the child says, "okay," then there's no issue. If a child wants something and gets a parent to say, "okay," "sure," or "no problem," then there is no sweat. The child smiles, is glad to have gotten what she or he wanted, and all is well. But what happens if a parent says, "no"? Or if your child ignores, defies, or argues with a request?

Behind most (if not all) "nos" is some kind of fear, or worry, or competing need. Our kid asks to stay up later. We are concerned that the child will be a "bear" in the morning and so we say "no." Our 14-year-old wants to go to the mall with some friends. We fear that the teen may be harmed and so we say "no." You're just getting in the door after work. You no sooner get inside than your kid wants to know if you will take him to the store. Chances are, you will immediately feel a kind of "digging in," a sort of resistance. You just got home and now you are being asked to go out. The child has a need for something (a toy, a video, something for a school project). . .you have a need for something else (like rest, some food, etc.).

Now, you have every right to JUST SAY NO. That's okay. Let's face it, not everything is up for discussion. I'd be the last one to say that we have to talk about our fears or needs to get our 4-year-old to eat some veggies. However, I want you to begin to realize that some of the day to day "conflicts" with your child can become teaching moments.

Children need to learn that when they want something and another person says "no," chances are high that the other person is concerned about something or has competing needs. Instead of whining, begging, yelling, or throwing a tantrum, kids need to learn to discover what the other person fears or wants to resolve the conflict. Solving problems with another person means that you try to get what you want while paying attention to the concerns and needs of the other person. That is the heart of the matter. Let's go over some of the more important steps in teaching your child.

Step One: Learning to Express Needs in a Respectful Way

How would you like your child to ask for something? "Hey mom, I need to go to . . ." "Dad, drive me to Billy's!" "Dad, you've got to take me to school in 10 minutes." "Mom, give me 10 dollars for the movies." Most of us don't like being bossed around by our kids. I can't imagine you do, either. So Step One in problem solving is for your child to learn what you consider a respectful way to ask.

How would you like your child to make requests? Is "May I," "Please," "Is it okay if," or "If it's not a problem for you dad, could you . . ." what you'd like to hear? Then you need to teach your child that skill. As with all the other lessons I talk about in this book, learning how to make a request or begin a discussion is important. Your child may want something, but so do you. You probably want respect and maybe a bit of appreciation. There is nothing wrong (and a lot right) about making sure that your child addresses your need to be respected or appreciated when he or she wants something. Kids with ADHD (like other kids) need to learn how to be sensitive to the needs and feelings of others. You need to be your child's teacher.

What if My Kid Ignores My Requests to Be Asked in a Respectful Way?

Remember when I discussed Time Stands Still? If your child ignores your requests to be spoken to respectfully, let the child know that you aren't going to consider any request until the child apologizes, does something to make amends, and speaks to you respectfully. Kids with ADHD can be intense and demanding. However, they can also learn that if they are disrespectful, they are postponing getting what they want. They can learn that disrespect leads to a need for an apology, making up, and then starting all over again.

Step Two: Understanding the Concerns and Needs of Others

Okay. Let's say your child has asked for something in a way that is respectful. Great. Now what? Well, now is the part that gets personal. If this is one of those times that you'd like to do a bit of teaching, you'll need to ask yourself a couple of questions.

> Question one is: "Am I thinking about saying 'no' because I'm concerned about something?" (Here you are trying to figure out if the "no" would be because of some type of concern.)

> Question two is: "Am I thinking about saying 'no' because I need something from my child? (Here you are trying to figure out if a "no" would be because of some kind of need that you have.)

Check yourself out. Let's play out a couple of situations.

Your 14-year-old daughter is asking to go to the movies with friends. You are feeling the urge to say "no." You say, "I'm not sure about that." Instead of begging or whining, your child learns to ask a simple question. She asks, "What are you afraid of, Mom?" You ask yourself, "Okay, what am I worried will happen if I say yes?" . . . Here are some possible concerns:

- My child won't be safe.
- My child will hang out in a place where kids smoke or use drugs.
- My child will pick up some "bad habits" from watching a certain movie.

- My child won't get her homework done.
- My child will stay up too late and not get up for church the next day.

This list is by no means exhaustive, but it's a starting point. The first question that needs to be asked and answered if you're thinking "no" because of worry is, "What am I concerned will happen?" For example, maybe you are thinking "no" because you're concerned your child won't be safe. If that's the case, then that's where you and your child start the "problem-solving." The problem for your child has now become the following: "How can I go to the movie and respect Mom's worry that I won't be safe?"

At this point, you can pull out a piece of paper and write down possible ways to address your safety concerns and still allow the child to go to the movies. What are some options? You and your child can sit down and take turns generating possible solutions. If your child starts to insult you (says you are being stupid, etc., etc.), then just like before the child will need to regroup and apologize. The child needs to learn that insulting another person is not a good problem-solving strategy. As long as the child is being respectful, you can proceed to list possible solutions. Here are several possibilities:

1. There should be at least four kids going to the movies; Mom will drop off and pick up in the lobby of the theater.

2. Sally and I take a bus to the theater, and I bring my cell phone in case of trouble.

3. Mom drops off Sally and me and picks up in the lobby of the theater.

4. Mom watches the movie with me and my friends.

5. My 18-year-old brother goes with us.

6. Mom and Dad go to one movie; you and your friends go to another movie at the same theater. We go into the theater together and leave together.

The problem-solving phase requires that your child realizes that she needs to respect your concerns, while the child attempts to get what she wants. If you are not comfortable with Sally and your daughter taking the bus, then that option is out. The only way your daughter gets to go is if she agrees to an option that does address your concerns. You could decide that options 1, 4, 5, and 6 are okay with you. Your daughter could decide which of those choices she likes. The essential lesson is this: In solving life problems, a person needs to address the concerns of parents, friends, teachers, co-workers, employers, spouse, or partner.

Let's say the worry is that if your daughter goes to the movie she will not complete her homework. If that's the case, then the problem for your child to solve is: "How can I go to the movie and also address Dad's concern that I won't do my homework?"

Some options to consider might include:

1. I do all my homework before going to the movie.
2. I do half my homework before the movie, and complete the other half on Sunday before I get to watch television or do anything "fun."
3. I promise to do my homework sometime before the weekend is over.

Let's say that you're okay with options 1 and 2. Then those are the choices from which your child can pick. Or, she can come up with another solution that will address your concern that homework won't get completed.

What if I'm Not Afraid? What if It's Just That I Don't Feel Like Saying "Yes"?

Not all requests meet with a parental "no" because of worry. Sometimes, the parent is feeling fatigued, burdened, or has some other need. If that is the case, your child needs to learn to ask question two: "Mom, is there anything I can do for you so you'll let me do (whatever), or so that you'll do (whatever) for me?" This question is designed to help your child figure out what you need so that you will say "yes." If fear is not part of the reason that you are saying "no" to a request, then chances are you have a need that should be addressed. Let's go back to the movie request.

What if the reason you are saying "no" to the movie request is because you feel tired . . . you feel like a slave to your kids . . . you feel as though you are the only person that does anything. So you ask yourself, "What do I need?" or "What does my child need to do so I'd be okay with taking her to the movies?" Instead of saying, "No . . . Mom's too tired," you could say the following:

> "I could really use a break before dinner. I wanted to unwind and watch a program that I taped. I was going to try to watch it after dinner, but if you'll help me prepare the meal, I'll take you and Sally to the movie. Here's what I want you to do. I'd like you to make the spaghetti and heat the sauce. First, I want you to fill this large pot with water and wait for it to boil. Once it starts to boil, let me know."

After the water boils and your daughter comes to you, you continue your instructions:

> "Okay, the next part of your job is to put a box of spaghetti in the pot and set the timer for 10 minutes. I also want you to heat the sauce that I've put in this pot on the stove. I don't want you to leave the kitchen, because you have to stir the pots to make sure the spaghetti doesn't stick and the sauce doesn't burn. Any questions? Okay then, we have a deal. You take care of dinner prep while I watch my program and I'll take you to the movie."

In this situation, the daughter was able to take care of her need by paying attention to her mom's need for some rest and relaxation. A pretty common parent need is the need for some help with the family's work. However, there is another need most parents have: They need to feel loved, "wanted," or appreciated by their child.

Let me tell you a brief story. I worked with a family who was struggling with their teenager's desire to spend every waking moment with his friends. The parents tried to do the best they could to get him to his friends' homes. However, one particular weekend the father said "no" to his son, telling him he couldn't go anywhere that weekend. The boy went "nuts." He'd done everything that he was supposed to, hadn't gotten into any trouble at school, so "WHY, WHY, WHY?!!!!!" couldn't he go out? However, the teen tried to solve the problem like a "baby," failing to realize that his dad must have wanted or was concerned about something to have said "no." After the dust settled, the teen learned that the simple reason his father wanted him home was that his dad missed spending time with him.

Although the father had to accept that his son needed to spend time with friends, his son learned that he had to become aware of his dad's needs, too. In this case, the father and son decided to plan some time for skiing together (with mutual family friends), so they could spend time going on some "runs" together and the son could continue to develop the friendships that were so important to him.

The sense of loss that a parent feels over the limited time spent with a child (particularly during the teenage years) is common, but it is not just a problem for the parent. Although teenagers will spend the vast majority of their time talking, instant messaging, visiting, and traveling with their friends, spending some time with parents remains important for the child's development during adolescence. Without any social or recreational contact with parents during adolescence, the parent–teen relationship deteriorates and conflict over typical teenage requests commonly escalates. Consequently, although parents need to be mindful that their teen's involvement with peers is an important developmental step, the lack of any type of parent–teen social or recreational involvement does not provide a foundation for maintaining an effective teaching role for parents through the teenage years.

HOMEWORK

The basics of solving problems between two people involves recognizing and respecting each person's needs and concerns. This is an important lesson for anyone to learn and apply. As is true with any lesson I discuss in this book, learning takes practice. Before you begin teaching this new skill, let your child know that you want to teach him or her another way to talk about problems. Tell the child your version of the story about how babies get what they want by crying, whining, and yelling, but as we grow up, we all have to learn a more "grown-up" way. Then sit down with them and use your variation of the Problem Worksheet that follows.

Problem Worksheet

What does your child want? _____

Why are you inclined to say "No"?

Is it a need? Ask yourself, "What do I want?" List it below.

_____

_____

Is it a concern? Ask yourself, "What am I afraid of?" List it below.

_____

_____

Solving this problem means that you and your child will need to take care of what the child needs, as well as your needs and concerns.

So, what ideas do you and your child have that work to solve this problem?

_____

_____

_____

_____

_____

After you list around six ideas, stop and cross out any that you (or your child) are not comfortable with, and select a solution from what remains. If you've crossed everything out, take a little time off (half an hour or so), and try again.

211

10

Parents Are People Too!

In this lesson, I shift focus a bit. Now that you understand that ADHD is a health problem (just like diabetes, anemia, and other medical conditions that can affect how a person acts), I hope you can use this knowledge and channel your energies into the gradual process of helping your child improve his or her behavior a little bit each day. I reviewed the importance of both the careful use of medication and of maintaining a balanced diet that includes eating protein in the morning and at lunchtime. I talked about establishing family rules that teach kids that in life, you get what you earn. I examined strategies designed to promote your child's sensitivity by encouraging the child to make amends when the child makes mistakes and to solve problems by learning about the needs and fears of others. Above it all, I stress the importance of demonstrating to your child each and every day that she or he is loved and is special to you.

So, what about you? Chances are that since your child has been born you have spent many (if not all) of your waking hours trying to keep the child out of harms way. Trying to figure out strategies to help your child get organized, stay on top of responsibilities, remember what he or she has been told, etc., etc., etc. In essence, you have played the role of your child's "brain" for as long as your child has been alive. That is a very, very, very draining job. When was the last time you sat down and planned some quality "unwind" time for yourself? Let's think about that for a bit.

A long time ago, in a lifetime far, far away, you were just yourself. You were a person trying to figure out a way to survive, have a bit of fun, and feel halfway decent about who you are. Okay, so you're a bit older now. However, that doesn't change the fact that you still need to have a bit of fun and feel halfway decent about yourself. In this lesson, I share a couple of parent "antidepressant" activities for you to consider. I hope you take the lessons in this chapter to heart. *If you are physically and mentally drained, it is unlikely you'll have the strength to teach your child any of the lessons in this book.*

ANTIDEPRESSANT ACTIVITIES FOR ADULTS

1. Each Day, Do at Least Three Things Just Because You Like to Do Them.

Let's start with this. I have to say that in my decades as a psychologist I've heard many people tell me that they spend their days doing all sorts of things for other people and feel exhausted and massively depressed.

So, the first idea that I want you to consider is how every day you can do a couple of activities that you enjoy.

Typically, when people hear this they think that I'm a doctor who is out of touch with reality. No, I really don't think that a single mother of six kids is going to easily find a way (or the desire) to hit that "abs" class at the "Y" three nights a week. I mean, that's great if you can get coverage for the kids. What I'm talking about are the "simple" pleasures in life.

I'm talking about getting some help from your kids so you can watch *your* favorite show. I'm talking about munching on a warm bagel in the morning with a bit of peanut butter and honey on it. I'm talking about putting your favorite tape or CD on the stereo and listening to it as you make dinner. I'm talking about reading a little bit of the Bible, the Koran, or some other inspirational book during a break at work. I'm talking about saving your pennies and picking up a magazine that you like and reading it during lunch. I'm talking about going to the library or one of those mega bookstores (with or without the kids), settling into a chair, sipping a mochaccino, and reading while the kids explore the world of books. I'm talking about e-mailing a friend. I'm talking about "surfing" the Internet. I'm talking about munching on some fries on the way home from work. I'm talking about a Snicker's Marathon bar that you look forward to in the mid-afternoon. I'm talking about an exercise that you enjoy. I can go on and on (my patients tell me that I certainly

can) . . . but I think you know what I mean. Be deliber-
ate. Make a point of picking out three things you will
do today just because you like them. Do this every
day. Believe me, it helps.

2. Protein is Important for Parents Too! Grab at Least 20 Grams for Breakfast and for Lunch.

Let's be honest. You'll never make it on coffee, ciga-
rettes, and donuts. There is no way that skipping protein at breakfast will gear you up for success. You know
the routine. You're too busy with the kids to eat in
the morning. So you gulp some coffee on the road. By
9:00 a.m., you hit the wall. You have another cup of
coffee (or other caffeine drink), plus some carbs (donut,
bagel, muffin). Perhaps you add some nicotine to the
mix. Maybe you kid yourself and think that a glass of
juice for breakfast will do the trick. That's a step in
the right direction, but it's really just more sugar with
none of the nutrition needed to fuel your decision-
making brain. So far, your body has not consumed
anywhere near the 20–30 grams or so that it needs to
fuel your brain.

Then lunch hits. Maybe you are weight conscious,
so you do the salad thing. You know protein is important, so maybe you add some eggs or a little tuna. Or
you eat a little yogurt. Check the fine print on the
carton. It's unlikely that you are anywhere near the
20–30 grams of protein that you need. Chances are
high that this afternoon, you'll feel mentally drained

and physically fatigued. Not a great state to be in when you and the kids meet up again at home.

Maybe you couldn't care less about weight and so you pack it in at lunch. Mega-sized meal at Burger World. The foot-long sub, packed with cheese and meat. The leisurely lunch at the nearby pasta place, with huge servings of spaghetti and meatballs. If you've skipped or skimped at breakfast, these types of meals are likely to leave you mentally exhausted and they certainly don't set the stage for effective functioning at work or at home.

The bottom line is that all the information about the importance of protein at breakfast and at lunch isn't just for the kids. Grab a soy-based protein shake if your appetite is low in the morning. There are plenty on the market that don't taste like chalk. Take a little time at night and make some breakfast brownies or muffins with the kids (pick your favorite recipe and add enough soy protein so that each brownie or muffin has at least five grams of protein). Snag one of those with a protein shake, and you're covered for the morning.

Can't find the time to bake? That's okay. Boil a bunch of eggs at night and store them in the fridge. You can munch on a couple in the morning. Hey, you don't even need to eat the yellow part (the protein's in the whites). In a time crunch? Roll up a little boiled ham, chicken breast, or turkey breast with a slice of cheese and walk out the door munching. Not only will these strategies help you feel awake in the morning at work, they'll prevent the fatigue that hits many of us after lunch. Besides, feeling well is part of the plan for you!

3. Everybody (Even Parents) Needs a Dream.

I believe it was those famous philosophers, The Rolling Stones, who once sang, "lose your dreams and you will lose your mind." I think there's something to that one. Part of what keeps life interesting is "the pursuit of happiness." Here's antidepressant idea number three: make a wish list of sorts. Here are a dozen prompts to get you started. Complete the sentences with whatever comes to mind:

If I weren't so old, I'd like to _____

Before I get "over the hill," I want to _____

If I weren't so afraid, I'd _____

Even though it's silly, I like _____

There is nothing like _____

If I had an extra $20, I'd _____

I sure would like it if my dad and I could _____

I sure would like it if my mom and I could _____

I sure would like it if my spouse or friend and I could _____

I always wanted to teach my kid to _____

I always wanted to learn to _____

When I look around my house or apartment I wish I had the energy to _____

These aren't the only prompts you can use, but try these and see what happens. Beginning something new provides a source of energy that can make life much less burdensome.

4. Save Some Time for Those You Love.

If you are married, are involved in a loving relationship, are close to members of your extended family, or have friendships, make sure that you cherish them. These are the primary sources of energy that will keep you afloat in the tough times. Here are a few suggestions on how to keep these connections alive:

- Each day, ask yourself: "What did I do to show my spouse, love, friend (etc.) that they were important to me?" Just as we need three meals of food every day, your spouse or loved one could use three "love" meals. Think about what spells love to your spouse or loved one (ask if you need to, it's okay). A lot of us walk around feeling unappreciated for our efforts. It's often not appreciated because it doesn't translate to "love." Working in a factory all day long might be your way of saying "I love you" to your family, but your wife might spell love as, "he tucks the kids in at night so I can finish the laundry." Think about it. Find a way to do three loving acts. You'll be amazed with the results.
- Each week, spend part of at least one day alone with your "love" doing something that the two of you enjoy. It doesn't matter if it boils down to munching on a bowl of popcorn while watching reruns of the "Andy Griffith Show" (one of my and my wife's favorite evening activities). What counts is that the two of you are together, and it's your time to enjoy as you please.

- Each season, try to go on an overnight trip away from the kids. Because we all need this kind of rejuvenation, relatives and friends often exchange babysitting for each other. Even one night away somewhere close to home is rejuvenating, and it's easier to get "coverage" for the kids if it's close by and you're only going away for one night.

5. Don't Isolate Yourself and Try to Raise Kids With ADHD Without Help.

There are some tasks in life that we can't do alone. Successfully raising kids with ADHD is one of them. To help your child succeed at home, at school, on the playground, and eventually in the workplace and in adult relationships, you need assistance. Establishing a relationship with health care professionals who are knowledgeable about the various types of treatments needed by patients with ADHD is an important first step. If the only type of treatment that your child is receiving is medication, then you need to identify other resources in your community. As I stress throughout this book, there are many, many lessons that medications cannot teach.

A good place to start is by asking your child's pediatrician for recommendations for a psychologist or other mental health professional who specializes in the treatment of ADHD. Another useful strategy is to contact the national organization for individuals with ADHD (Children and Adults with Attention-Deficit/

Hyperactivity Disorder: CH.A.D.D.). This group maintains a web site (www.chadd.org) and can also be contacted by phone (301-306-7070). CH.A.D.D. provides educational materials and can assist you in learning about local "chapters" that conduct educational and support meetings. Both the national and local CH.A.D.D. organizations can help you learn about support groups in your community. Members of these support groups are likely to be able to provide the names of individuals who specialize in the treatment of ADHD. Such individuals will be able to assist you in developing a treatment plan for your child that is much more comprehensive than medication alone.

If you are unable to identify a specialist in your region through support groups, a university medical center may be of assistance. Most university-based medical centers have child and adolescent psychiatrists and psychologists who either treat ADHD or can assist you in identifying such specialists in your community. Another resource that can help you locate a specialist is a graduate program in Clinical Psychology at a college or university near your community.

HOMEWORK

Homework? What homework? This lesson was about some R&R for you. Take a little time for yourself. Remember that simple pleasures can be the best.

11

It Don't Come Easy

Whenever I finish reading a parenting book, I typically have a sense that something is missing. No matter how sensible the advice, no matter how practical the ideas, I recognize that the learning process is not easy. You know that, too. I typically find myself wondering, "Is it really that easy?" Well, at this point, you have finished reading *my* parenting book. However, it is very unlikely that your child is "all better." I hope that some of the lessons shared in this book are taking hold. Maybe your child isn't as prone to anger. Maybe he is doing better in school. Maybe it doesn't take a dozen reminders for her to do what she is supposed to do. However, the odds are that your child still whines, gripes, loses his cool, and tries to avoid tasks that require sustained mental effort at times. So it makes little sense to pretend that when parents complete my 10-session program, "all is well."

Having taught hundreds of classes for parents, I recognize that most parents have difficulties putting lessons into action. Chances are, so are you. In this lesson, I share with you some of the common problems experienced by parents in my program. I also give you some ideas for overcoming them. Let's start by reviewing where you are in the change process.

When you began reading this book, you completed a "Top 40" list of improvements that you wanted to see in your child. Since that time, I hope that you've learned about the causes of ADHD, the importance of nutrition, the need for a supportive educational plan, the benefits of medication, as well as other strategies to improve the lives of children and teens with ADHD. Most important, I ask you to think about family life and how children learn new skills.

In this book, I emphasize that learning requires several steps. First, you must plan what you want to teach and give the child "advance notice." Second, you should not try to teach a new lesson in the middle of a conflict situation. Third, the child needs to be told (simply and directly) what you want him or her to do or not do. Fourth, the child needs to realize that if he or she does not do what was required by you, there will be specific consequences (most commonly, that life is "on hold" until the child does what was requested and something in addition to "make up" for the behavior). Fifth, if the child displayed anger toward you, was disrespectful, or whined and gave you a hard time, the child needs to apologize, do some kind of "make up," and then follow your directions.

When we considered the lessons you wanted to teach your child, I asked you to analyze your lesson plan and think about the sequence of events that took place. What did you say to your child? What did the child do? What were the consequences of the child's actions? So often children persist in their old ways by arguing, whining, avoiding, and refusing to cooperate. If the result of the defiance or avoidance leads you to back off and the child does not have to comply, no improvement will occur. Time and again, I have seen that no change occurs in the child if parents were not clear about what they wanted or if there were no consequences for the child's actions (other than some parental lecture).

In this book, I ask you to reflect on your family life. I stress the importance of setting aside some time each day to give your child the gift of your attention. I ask you to consider establishing a "non-aggression pact" in your family so your home could become a place where aggression, teasing, and sarcasm are not "okay." I also emphasize the importance of weekly parent "planning time," a scheduled time when you think about what you are trying to teach and what changes need to be made in your lesson plan. I ask you to consider teaching your child how to solve problems by learning to discover the concerns and needs of others. Finally, I discuss the obvious fact that if you are going to be an effective parent, you need love, companionship, fun, and a healthy diet.

225

My question now is, "HOW ARE YOU DOING?" Is your family moving in the right direction? I hope so. However, chances are there is still room for improvement. Take a few minutes and complete the Parenting Program Checklist. It should give you a better idea about what needs to be done now.

Parenting Program Checklist

(Place a check under yes or no.)

Treatment Plan: The Basics   **YES   NO**

My child has been evaluated by a physician
for other medical problems that can cause
ADHD "symptoms."

My child has been evaluated for visual deficits
by an optometrist or ophthalmologist, and for
auditory deficits by an audiologist.

My child is being treated for ADHD with
medication or EEG biofeedback.

My child eats at least 20 grams of protein

    at breakfast.
    at lunch.

My child sleeps at least eight hours per night.

My child has been referred for evaluation
by the special education committee and an
educational plan has been established (or is
in the process of being developed).

My family has agreed to the Parent–Child
Non-Aggression Pact.

I plan weekly meetings to review goals for
my children.

Parenting Program Checklist

Treatment Plan: Skill Development   YES   NO

My child follows family rules:

> before school
> after school
> after dinner

When my child doesn't follow family
rules, I

> use "Time Stands Still."
> insist on an apology.
> insist on a "make up."
> insist on doing the required task or
> an acceptable alternative.

When my child displays inappropriately
intense anger, sadness, or anxiety, I

> use "Time Stands Still."
> insist on an apology.
> insist on a "make up."
> practice an appropriate method for
> expressing need, frustration, etc.

Parenting Program Checklist

Treatment Plan: Skill Development   YES   NO

My child solves problems by asking about my concerns and needs and "brainstorms" with me to find a solution.

My child is involved in activities that matter to his or her peers.

My child engages in conversations about topics of interest to others.

My child records daily activities and responsibilities on a board or other visual prompt.

I spend at least 15 minutes each day enjoying a recreational activity with my child.

Treatment Plan: Parent "Self-Care"

I do three things that I enjoy each day.

I eat at least 20 grams of protein

> at breakfast.
> at lunch.

I am currently working on achieving one of my "dreams."

I show my partner that she or he is loved by me in ways that "count" to <u>my partner</u>.

I sleep at least seven hours per night.

Now that you've finished the questionnaire, let's look at your answers. If you are following treatment plan recommendations for "The Basics" and "Parent Self-Care" but are having specific "Skill Development Problems," take a few minutes to consider your lesson plan. For those skills that are not progressing, have you told the child what is required? Are you using motivational strategies like "Time Stands Still," combined with "apologies" and "amends"? If not, meet with your child, review your "lesson plan," and start again.

If you are not following treatment plan recommendations for "The Basics" and "Parent Self-Care" sections, welcome to the club. These are the two areas where parenting efforts commonly bog down. However, they cannot be ignored if you are to succeed in your efforts to help your child. Following are some common problems experienced by the parents who have participated in my groups along with some suggestions on what to do about them.

Problem 1: Your child continues to demonstrate poor response to "first line" treatments for ADHD (i.e., stimulant medications) and does not seem to be learning much from your efforts to use the lessons in this book.

Suggestion: Make sure the child has been tested for other conditions listed on the questionnaire, and that you have addressed dietary and sleep problems. If you have ignored this important step, please reconsider. Before you start combining medications, shifting to "non-ADHD" medications, or concluding that your child is emotionally disturbed, have your child tested (and treated) for other medical conditions and address any dietary or sleep problems.

Problem 2: Your child is not responding to stimulant medication, but there are no other medical, nutritional, or sleep issues. The physician has increased the dose but that appears to be making the situation worse.

Suggestion: Consider a Quantitative Electroencephalographic (QEEG) evaluation for your child. Studies published by my clinic as well as by researchers at New York University's Brain Research Laboratory, the University of Tennessee, and the University of Woolongong (Australia) have noted that underactivity in the frontal and central, midline regions of the brain is a common characteristic of ADHD patients who respond to stimulant medications. However, this research has indicated that approximately 10%–20% of ADHD patients do not demonstrate such "underactivity" and do not respond well to stimulant medications. Consequently, an alternative to a trial and error medication approach would be to conduct a QEEG evaluation. If underactivity is not noted, consider use of a non-stimulant ADHD medication (Strattera) or an antihypertensive medication (Catapres or Tenex).

Problem 3: Your child appears to be improving with medication but is still not completing schoolwork or homework and is disruptive in class. The school district thinks your child is lazy and is resistant to conducting an evaluation.

Suggestion: Write a letter to the chairperson of the Committee on Special Education or to whomever is responsible for conducting evaluations and coordinating the educational plans of children with disabilities in your child's school district. Inform them that your child has been diagnosed with ADHD (provide written documentation by the health care provider who made the diagnosis). Request that an evaluation for learning disabilities and functional impairments associated with ADHD be conducted (as mandated by the educational laws in every state). The district must respond to such a written request. After the evaluation is completed, an IEP or 504 Plan will be developed to help with any learning disabilities or functional problems. However, these plans frequently do not address motivational issues. Assistance may be provided (in the form of "resource room teachers," class notes, study guides, etc.), but one of the core symptoms of ADHD (avoids tasks that require sustained mental effort) is often ignored.

To address such motivational issues, I strongly recommend that (at minimum) weekly progress reports be provided to parents. These reports need to specifically list any missing assignments so the child can be required to complete them over the weekend (even if they "don't count" for a grade). In addition, I recommend that the child be required to complete additional assignments so the child will realize that avoidance of work will not be successful and will only lead to "extra" assignments. Should these teacher reports indicate disrespect or defiance of the teacher, then the child should be required to apologize and make amends (just as the child must do at home).

Problem 4: Everything seems to be going along fine until the evening. There appear to be no adverse effects because of your child's use of a sustained-release stimulant medication during the daytime. However, at night your child is arguing, throwing tantrums, refusing to follow your rules, and won't go to sleep.

Suggestion: There are medical, nutritional, and psychological strategies to consider. Medical interventions that seem to help with this type of problem include use of antihypertensive medications (such as Catapres) in the evening to reduce aggression and promote onset of sleep. Monitoring dietary habits in the evening may reveal that your child continues to eat in the evening or to drink stimulatory (high sugar or caffeinated) beverages, which can postpone sleep onset. Eliminating consumption of carbohydrates and "sugary" drinks after dinner may prove helpful. Parenting strategies (e.g., needing to apologize and do some type of corrective action the next afternoon before being allowed to play) also may help.

Problem 5: You are arguing with your child all the time and are too overwhelmed to schedule a "parent meeting" to think about what you should do.

Suggestion: Let's start with some basic care for yourself. If you are "relapsing" and arguing like crazy, nothing positive is likely to happen until you get squared away. So, trust that good ideas for helping your child will come to mind after you get some rest, start eating 20 grams of protein at breakfast and lunch, and begin doing things that you enjoy each day. One of my favorite acronyms from Alcoholics Anonymous is HALT (Hungry, Angry, Lonely, Tired). Essentially, the idea is that a person will relapse into old, destructive habits when they are hungry, angry, lonely, or tired. You're only human. If you are feeling as though things are out of control, begin with yourself and start to address your hunger, anger, loneliness, and fatigue. Then return to this book, review those lessons that cover the "skill development" areas you want to work on, and get started. If this doesn't work and you continue to feel overwhelmed, schedule an appointment for yourself with your doctor. There may be undiagnosed medical problems that are getting in the way. Or as you may have suspected, you, too, may have ADHD and need effective treatment.

Final Thoughts

Buried somewhere in the pages of a typical book are an author's "acknowledgments" of the people who helped the author. However, because those who helped me deserve to be noted, I include my "thank-yous" here, rather than in a page before the Table of Contents that most of us overlook. There is no way that I could possibly do my work alone. I am grateful for those who helped me and thought you might like to know who they are.

First, I want to express my gratitude to my wife, Donna. It has been said that with love, all things are possible. Without her love and support, this book would have never been written. She encouraged me to write this parenting book and tolerated the endless hours that I worked on the manuscript. She also served as the first "editor" of this book, helping me to translate the clinic's approach into a series of lessons that could be applied by those raising children and teens with ADHD. I want to express my unending appreciation to my wife for her love, support, and honest critique of my work.

I'd also like to express my thanks to my parents. Although both of my parents were somewhat apologetic that they had never gone to college, they possessed wisdom and the kind of "common sense" that has served me well. My mom was the person who taught me the value of Work for Play, and it was dad's patience in the midst of turmoil that served as a model for the problem-solving strategies I use in my clinical work. I'll never forget sitting at the kitchen table going over options to solve a problem, as he jotted down ideas on a dinner napkin.

Next, I'd like to express my appreciation to my professors, supervisors, and mentors, beginning with Dr. Paul Toomin, who taught me that scientific research requires more than a series of "pilot" studies. I'd also like to thank Dr. Doug Lowe, who introduced me to the world of physiology and brain–behavior relationships; and Dr. Joel Lubar, who showed me how the brains of patients with ADHD could begin to "heal." I'd also like to express my appreciation to the training staff at the Philadelphia Child Guidance Clinic for helping me develop my skills in parent counseling and family therapy. I'll never forget my pre-dawn drives to the Children's Hospital of Philadelphia (CHOP), the countless late-night hours viewing videotapes of treatment sessions, and the opportunity to learn from Dr. Minuchin, Dr. Whitaker, Dr. Covelman, Barbara Forbes-Bryant, Jamshed Morenas,

Jorge Colapinto, and the rest of the highly talented and greatly respected staff.

I'd also like to express my appreciation to my patients and their parents for having the courage to believe that change was possible, despite years of disappointment and frustration. I truly believe that my patients with ADHD are the nation's diamonds in the rough. They are extraordinary individuals who have the potential to make significant contributions to our society. My job, and yours, is to try to make sure that they are not discarded.

Finally, I want to thank God for giving me the ability to learn and share knowledge about ways to improve the lives of my patients. Before each of my scientific presentations, I close my eyes, imagine one of the thousands of children I have treated, and ask God to guide me as I speak. As I wrote this book, the faces and stories of many of these children came to mind. I can only hope that the lessons they taught me can, in turn, help you as you raise your child.

Best Wishes!

Dr. Monastra

Supplemental Readings

In this section, I provide you with a listing of books and scientific articles that can provide more detailed information about a topic covered in a particular lesson. In some ways, this list will be similar to the kind that a teacher in high school or college might include for students who want to learn more about what was covered in a particular class. The supplemental readings have been separated by lesson number so you can easily find further readings on subjects covered in these lessons.

INTRODUCTION

For those of you who are interested in the scientific paper on the parenting program, the reference is as follows:

Monastra, V. J., Monastra, D., & George, S. (2002). The effects of stimulant therapy, EEG biofeedback, and parenting style on the primary symptoms of attention-deficit/hyperactivity disorder. *Applied Psychophysiology and Biofeedback, 27* (4), 231–249.

Lesson 2

Amen, D. G. (1998). *Change your brain, change your life*. New York: Times Books.

Barkley, R. A. (1998). *Attention-deficit/hyperactivity disorder: A handbook for diagnosis and treatment* (2nd ed.). New York: Guilford Press.

Biederman, J., Faraone, S. V., & Lapey, K. (1992). Comorbidity of diagnosis in attention deficit/hyperactivity disorder. In G. Weiss (Ed.), *Child and adolescent psychiatric clinics of North America* (pp. 335–360). Philadelphia: Saunders.

Biederman, J., Faraone, S. V., Mick, E., Spencer, T., Wilens, T., Kiely, K., et al. (1995). High risk for attention deficit hyperactivity disorder among children of parents with childhood onset of the disorder: A pilot study. *American Journal of Psychiatry, 152,* 431–435.

Blum, K., Braverman, E. R., Holder, J. M., Lubar, J. F., Monastra, V. J., Miller, D., et al. (2000). Reward deficiency syndrome: A biogenetic model for the diagnosis and treatment of impulsive, addictive, and compulsive behaviors. *Journal of Psychoactive Drugs, 32*(Suppl.), 1–112.

Chabot, R. J., diMichele, F., Prichep, L., & John, E. R. (2001). The clinical role of computerized EEG in the evaluation and treatment of learning and attention disorders in children and adolescents. *Journal of Neuropsychiatry and Clinical Neurosciences, 13,* 171–186.

Clarke, A. R., Barry, R. J., McCarthy, R., & Selikowitz, M. (2001). EEG-defined subtypes of children with attention-deficit/hyperactivity disorder. *Clinical Neurophysiology, 112,* 2098–2105.

Clarke, A. R., Barry, R. J., McCarthy, R., & Selikowitz, M. (2001). Electroencephalogram differences in two subtypes of attention-deficit/hyperactivity disorder. *Psychophysiology, 38,* 212–221.

Dougherty, D. D., Bonab, A. A., Spencer, T. J., Rauch, S. L., Madras, B. K., & Fishman, A. J. (1999). Dopamine transporter density in patients with attention deficit hyperactivity disorder. *Lancet, 354,* 1461–1462.

Giedd, J. N., Blumenthal, J., Molloy, E., & Castellanos, F. X. (2001). Brain imaging of attention deficit/hyperactivity disorder. *Annals of the New York Academy of Sciences, 931,* 33–49.

Monastra, V. J., Lubar, J. F., Linden, M., VanDeusen, P., Green, G., Wing, W., et al. (1999). Assessing attention-deficit/hyperactivity disorder via quantitative electroencephalography: An initial validation study. *Neuropsychology, 13*(3), 424–433.

Monastra, V. J., Lubar, J. F., & Linden, M. (2001). The development of a quantitative electroencephalographic scanning process for attention-deficit/

hyperactivity disorder: Reliability and validity studies. *Neuropsychology, 15*(1), 136–144.

Swanson, J. M., & Castellanos, F. X. (2002). Biological bases of ADHD: Neuroanatomy, genetics and pathophysiology. In P. S. Jensen & J. R. Cooper (Eds.), *Attention deficit hyperactivity disorder: State of the science: Best practices* (pp. 7–1 to 7–20). Kingston, NJ: Civic Research Institute.

Lesson 3

Chabot, R. J., Orgill, A. A., Crawford, G., Garris, M., & Serfontein, G. (1999). Behavioral and electrophysiologic predictors of treatment response to stimulants in children with attention disorders. *Journal of Child Neurology, 14*(6), 343–351.

Clarke, A. R., Barry, R. J., McCarthy, R., & Selikowitz, M. (2002). EEG differences between good and poor responders to methylphenidate and dexamphetamine in children with attention-deficit/ hyperactivity disorder. *Clinical Neurophysiology, 113*, 194–205.

DuPaul, G. J., Barkley, R. A., & Connor, D. R. (1998) Stimulants. In R. A. Barkley (Ed.), *Attention deficit hyperactivity disorder: A handbook for diagnosis and treatment* (pp. 510–551). New York: Guilford Press.

Greenhill, L. L. (2002). Stimulant medication treatment of children with attention deficit hyperactivity disorder. In P. S. Jensen & J. R. Cooper (Eds.),

Attention deficit hyperactivity disorder: State of the science: Best practices (pp. 9–1 to 9–27). Kingston, NJ: Civic Research Institute.

Lubar, J. F. (2003). Neurofeedback for the management of attention deficit disorders. In M. S. Schwartz & F. Andrasik (Eds.), *Biofeedback: A practitioner's guide* (pp. 409–437). New York: Guilford Press.

Monastra, V. J. (2003). Clinical applications of electroencephalographic biofeedback. In M. S. Schwartz & F. Andrasik (Eds.), *Biofeedback: A practitioner's guide* (pp. 380–463). New York: Guilford Press.

Pelham, W. E. (2002). Psychosocial interventions for ADHD. In P. S. Jensen & J. R. Cooper (Eds.), *Attention deficit hyperactivity disorder: State of the science: Best practices* (pp. 12–2 to 12–36). Kingston, NJ: Civic Research Institute.

Spencer, T., Biederman, J., & Wilens, T. (1996). Pharmacotherapy of ADHD: A literature review. *Journal of the American Academy of Child and Adolescent Psychiatry, 35,* 409–432.

Wilens, T. E. (2004). *Straight talk about psychiatric medications for kids.* New York: Guilford Press.

LESSON 4

Bruner, A.B., Joffe, A., Duggan, A. K., Casella, J. R., & Brandt, T. (1996). Randomized study of cognitive effects of iron supplementation in non-anemic, iron-deficit adolescent girls. *Lancet, 348,* 992–996.

Burgess, J. R., Stevens, L., Zhang, W., & Peck, L. (2000). Long-chain polyunsaturated fatty acids in children with attention-deficit hyperactivity disorder. *American Journal of Clinical Nutrition*, *71*(1), 327–330.

Egger, J., Stolla, A., & McEwen, L. M. (1992). Controlled trial of hyposensitization in children with food-induced hyperkinetic syndrome. *Lancet*, *339*, 1150–1153.

Fairbanks, V., & Beutler, E. (1995). Iron deficiency. In E. Beutler (Ed.), *Williams hematology* (5th ed., p. 495). New York: McGraw-Hill.

Feingold, B. F. (1975). *Why your child is hyperactive*. New York: Random House.

Fernstrom, J. D. (1983). Role of precursor availability in control of monoamine biosynthesis in the brain. *Physiology Review*, *63*, 484–546.

Fernstrom, J. D. (1994). Dietary amino acids and brain function. *Journal of the American Dietetic Association*, *94*(1), 71–77.

Fernstrom, J. D. (1999). Effects of dietary polyunsaturated fatty acids on neuronal function. *Lipids*, *34*, 161–169.

Fierke, C. (2000). Function and mechanism of zinc. *Journal of Nutrition*, *130*, 1437S–1446S.

Fischer, K., Colombani, P. C., Langhans, W., & Wenk, C. (2001). Cognitive performance and its relationship with postprandial metabolic changes after ingestion of different macronutrients in the morning. *British Journal of Nutrition, 85,* 393–405.

Hambridge, M. (2000). Human zinc deficiency. *The Journal of Nutrition, 130*(Suppl. 5), 1344S–1349S.

Hartsough, C. S., & Lambert, N. M. (1985). Medical factors in hyperactive and normal children: Prenatal, developmental and health history findings. *American Journal of Orthopsychiatry, 55,* 190–210.

Kozielec, T., & Starobrat-Hermelin, B. (1994). Deficiency of certain trace elements in children with hyperactivity. *Polish Journal of Psychiatry, 28,* 345–353.

Kozielec, T., & Starobrat-Hermelin, B. (1997). Assessment of magnesium levels in children with attention-deficit/hyperactivity disorder. *Magnesium Research, 10*(2), 143–148.

Mattes, J. A., & Gittelman, R. (1981). Effects of artificial food coloring in children with hyperactive symptoms: A critical review and results of a controlled study. *Archives of General Psychiatry, 38,* 714–718.

Mitchell, E. A., Aman, M. G., Turbott, S. H., & Manku, M. (1987). Clinical characteristics and serum essential fatty acid levels in hyperactive children. *Clinical Pediatrics, 26,* 406–411.

Oski, F. A., Honig, A. S., Helu, B., & Howanitz, P. (1983). Effect of iron therapy on behavior performance in non-anemic, iron-deficient infants. *Pediatrics, 71*, 877–880.

Rowe, K. S. (1988). Synthetic food colorings and "hyperactivity": A double blind crossover study. *Australian Paediatric Journal, 24*(2), 143–147.

Rowe, K. S., & Rowe, K. J. (1994). Synthetic food coloring and behavior: A dose response effect in a double-blind, placebo-controlled, repeated-measures study. *The Journal of Pediatrics, 125*(5), 691–698.

Schmidt, M. H., Mocks, P., Lay, B., Eisert, H. G., Fojkar, R., Fritz-Sigmund, D., et al. (1997). Does oligoantigenic diet influence hyperactive/conduct-disordered children: A controlled trial. *European Child and Adolescent Psychiatry, 6*, 88–95.

Swanson, J. M., & Kinsbourne, M. (1980). Food dyes impair performance of hyperactive children on a laboratory learning test. *Science, 207*, 1485–1486.

Wurtman, R. J., & Wurtman, J. J. (Eds.). (1983). *Nutrition and the brain.* New York: Raven Press.

LESSON 8

Babyak, M., Blumenthal, J. A., & Herman, S. (2000). Exercise treatment for major depression: Maintenance of therapeutic benefit at 10 months. *Psychosomatic Medicine, 62*, 633–638.

Blumenthal, J. A., Babyak, M. A., & Moore, K. A. (1999). Effects of exercise training on older people with major depression. *Archives of Internal Medicine, 159*, 2349–2356.

LESSON 11

Nadeau, K. G. (1995). *A comprehensive guide for attention deficit disorder in adults: Research, diagnosis and treatment.* New York: Brunner/Mazel.

Ratey, J. J., Greenberg, M. S., & Lindem, K. J. (1991). Combination of treatments for attention deficit/hyperactivity disorder in adults. *Journal of Nervous and Mental Disease, 179*, 699–701.

Index

251

non-medication, 67–69
problem solving in, 229
psychological, 37–38
skill development in, 228

Underarousal, of frontal lobes, 29–30, 34
USDA *National Nutrient Database for Standard Reference*, 82, 85

Vision impairment, ADHD comparison with, 125

Wants
disrespect in asking, 203
earning, 133, 134, 163, 184
expressing in respectful way, 202–203
identification of, 180–182

needs of others and, 200, 201, 202
ways to get, 199–200
Wellbutrin, 63
Work for Play plan, 146–147, 157–159, 162
at after school care location, 158
earning in, 157, 158
organization of, 157–159
responsibilities in, 157, 158
Worry, in problem solving, 204–207

Zinc
deficiency of, 24, 28
enzyme development for neurotransmitters, 78
food log record of, 85
recommended dietary allowance for, 84
sources of, 78
Zoloft, 51, 64, 65, 187

About the Author

Vincent J. Monastra, PhD, is a clinical psychologist who serves as the director of the FPI Attention Disorders Clinic in Endicott, New York. Dr. Monastra is internationally recognized for his research examining neurophysiological characteristics of children and teens with ADHD and his treatment studies demonstrating the significance of parenting style, school intervention, nutrition, and EEG biofeedback in the overall care of these patients. He frequently lectures and conducts workshops at scientific conferences, schools, and public forums throughout the United States and Canada. His scientific awards include the President's Award and the Hans Berger Award, bestowed on him by the Association for Applied Psychophysiology and Biofeedback for his research with patients diagnosed with ADHD. Further information about Dr. Monastra's work is available at www.theADHDdoc.com.